CW00803025

INDIA

50 YEARS OF INDEPENDENCE: 1947-97

Status, Growth & Development

Volume 19

WOMEN WRITERS

Literary Interviews

RANAVIR RANGRA

B.R. PUBLISHING CORPORATION

[A Division of BRPC (India) Ltd.]

Delhi-110052

celebrating silver jubilee

Distributed by:
D.K. Publishers Distributors (P) Ltd.
1 Ansari Road, Darya Ganj
New Delhi-110 002
Phones: 326 1465, 327 8368
Fax: 091-011-326 4368

ISBN 81-7018-980-2 (Set)
ISBN 81-7018-999-3 (Vol. 19)

Published by:
B.R. Publishing Corporation
[A Division of BRPC (India) Ltd.]
A-6 Nimri Commercial Centre
Near Bharat Nagar, Ashok Vihar
Delhi-110 052
Phones: 743 0113, 714 3353
Fax: 091-011-745 2453
E-Mail: *brpcltd@del2.vsnl.net.in*

Laser Typeset by:
Veronica Grafic Arts
Delhi-110 034

Printed at:
Santosh Offset, Delhi-110035

PRINTED IN INDIA

On
The Golden Jubilee
of
India's Independence

Preface

It is not only the writer that gets churned from within and without during the creative act. The reader is also perturbed as he involves himself in the act of comprehension. What flows from the writer through his writing and what the reader already possesses take time and effort to come to a confluence. The reader has, at times, to grapple with the incoming substance with all his might to assimilate it. The process of comprehension does not end when we close the book after reading it, but continues at the subconscious level. The stronger the writing, the longer it stays with the reader and grows as he grows. The real culmination of any literary work takes place not in the pages of the book, but in the mind of the reader.

Some works set the reader on unending quests and when he fails to meet them despite his concerted effort, he looks to the writer for a hint to unravel the mystery surrounding it. Whenever he happens to meet the writer, he cannot resist the temptation to get a glimpse into his mind. Even if the elucidation offered by the writer is not found fully dependable and final, it does throw some light on the subtleties and proves helpful as such.

It is indeed the inquisitiveness as a reader that prompted me to approach writers for interviews on their writings. Various inquiries had been piling up in my mind while studying their literature. Though my constant grappling with them found answers to some of them in my own way, most of them continued staring me in the face. Whenever, I had a chance to meet a writer, I put my queries to him, as they occurred to me, unhesitatingly. At times, I did feel that my query seemed somewhat out of place, even silly, but spontaneous that it was, I did not suppress it. It was the greatness of the writers, I must own, that they not only consented to be interviewed, but also put up with my unpalatable questions and provided their replies.

The first collection of my literary interviews with writers in Hindi *Srijan Ki Manobhūmi*, which appeared in 1968 after about sixteen years of research, contained twenty-one interviews. Ten years later in 1978, another collection entitled *Sāhityik Sākshātkār*, containing forty-one interviews with twenty-nine Hindi writers, was published. Both the volumes were well received and my attempt to bridge the gap between the writer and the reader, as also the critic, was appreciated. This encouraged me to go ahead in this almost ignored field and extend my probe into the literatures of other Indian languages.

Further work in this field confirmed my earlier contention that 'the Indian literature, though written in different languages, is basically one' is not a mere slogan. It is a statement of cultural fact. I found unity of outlook amongst the Indian writers in different languages. They draw inspiration from a common source and share emotional as well as intellectual experiences. Their spiritual, philosophic and social background is almost identical. Indian literature finds an analogy in our traditional multi-wick oil-lamp, each wick representing the literature of a language. Lights from different wicks merge imperceptibly and produce unity with multiplied brightness. The interviews with Indian writers, contained in the next volume *Bhāratiya Sāhityakāron Se Sākshātkār* published in 1988, bring out this sense of unity. Its English edition *Interviews with Indian Writers*, brought out in 1992, contains my interviews with thirty-five writers of fifteen Indian languages, held from time to time. It is interesting to note that the first series of my interviews commenced with Jainendra Kumar in 1952 and, it may just be a coincidence, the last one concluded also with his interview in 1986. I have included in that volume both the interviews for a comparative study.

The present volume, an extension of the earlier ones, concentrates on women writers. It contains my sixteen interviews with writers of twelve Indian languages.

My main aim in these interviews has been to have and provide a glimpse into the creative mind of the writers. I have taken care to avoid unending argumentation with them as I soon learnt from experience that argumentation brings the discussion down to a conscious level. As it were, precious revelations emerge, when they do, from the depths of the subconscious.

Most of the interviews were taken at the writers' own places. Whether the interview was taken down or taped, its typed script was essentially prepared and shown to the writer for authentication to obviate any controversy. The cassettes of the interviews as well as the corrected and authenticated copies of the scripts are available in the repertory of the Indira Gandhi National Centre for the Arts, New Delhi, for researchers.

Though these interviews concentrate on the respective writings of the writers, some basic issues relating to the creative process come up again and again. Yet personal experiences of the interviewees during the act of creation have lent them new dimensions.

All the Indian writers, despite the fact that they write in different languages, belong to one *Sāraswata* family. In the Indian families, the age factor gains precedence even today. The interviews have therefore been arranged not alphabetically, but according to the dates of birth of the writers. This has resulted in not only harmonious knitting of the languages, but has also brought the contemporaries closer. Place and date of the interview has been recorded at the end.

The interviews were conducted in English, Hindi or the mother tongue of the writer according to their convenience. Where an interview was conducted in a language other than English an indication to this effect has been given.

These interviews have opened up for me at least new vistas of approaching and comprehending the Indian writers and their writings, and I do find myself richer. If others also find them useful, I shall indeed be gratified.

August 15, 1997 **RANAVIR RANGRA**

Contents

*Interviews conducted in languages other than English.

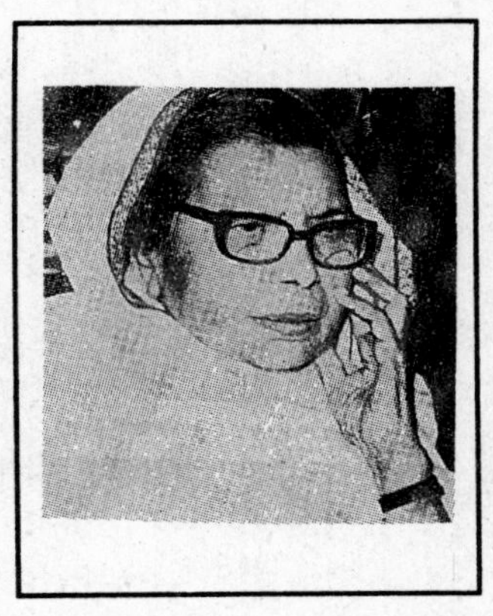

Mahadevi Varma

B. 26.3.1907, Farrukhabad; *d.* 11.9.1987; *mt.* Hindi; *edn.* M.A. (Sanskrit); *car.* Former Principal and Vice Chancellor, Mahila Vidyapith, Allahabad; *Awards & hons.* Mangalā Prasād Pāritoshik, Fellow, Sahitya Akademi, Bharatiya Jnanpith Award*, 1982, D. Litt. (Hon. cau.), Padmabhushan; *Pubs. Hindi poetry* Nīhār, 1930, Rashmī, 1932, Nīrajā, 1934, Yāmā*, 1951, Dīpashikhā, 1954, *essays* Shrinkhalā Kī Kadiyān, 1950, *reminiscences* Atita Ke Chalachitra, 1941, Smriti Kī Rekhāyen, 1947, Path Ke Sathī, 1956, *Lit. crit.* Sāhityakār Kī Āstha.

Burn On, O My Lamp, Without A Flicker

Mahadevi Verma is essentially a poetess of anguish, intense sorrow. Her poetry is the off-shoot of deep agony and life-long suffering. To her, life is a confluence of anguish and compassion, 'Life is, the lotus of separation/Born in pain and abiding in compassion'. She considers pain a poetry of life, capable of binding the whole world together, 'Burn on without a Flicker, O My Lamp'. She believes that merging his own life into the life of the universe, his own anguish into the universal anguish, just as a drop of water merges into the ocean, is the real deliverance for a poet.

Though pain was the subject of her poetry, she did not entertain any feeling of remorse towards pleasure. She would rather embrace sorrow than have the exhilaration of pleasure. Analysing the inclinations dominating her at the time of the creation of her anthologies entitled *Nihār* (Mist), *Rashmi* (Ray), *Nīrajā* (Lotus) and *Sāndhya-gīt* (Evening Song), she observes, "During the creation of *Nihār*, my feelings carried that kind of curiosity based on agony which rises in the mind of a child on seeing the far off unavailable golden dawn and also on the first sight of water cloud beyond his touch. *Rashmi* took shape when to me the very thought of emotion was dearer than its actual feeling. But *Nīrajā* and *Sāndhya-gīt* express that state of my mind in which my heart began experiencing the blending of pain and pleasure."

Appreciating the poetic genius of Mahadevi Varma, eminent Hindi poet Nirala rightly called her 'vīnāpāni' (Goddess Saraswati) of the magnificient temple of Hindi'. Her poetry transcends worldly achievements and fulfilments: 'Never talk of Union/I am in perpetual separation'. She values perseverance more than achievement, as she feels the very act of achieving, blunts the thrust of the effort. Like a real *Sadhika*, she wishes to remain thirsty, far from fulfilment: 'Don't give even an iota of contentment in my short life/Let my thirsty eyes fill the ocean of compassion.'

I chanced upon Mahadeviji when she visited Delhi last month and addressed a mammoth gathering on the cultural background of Hindi Literature in the University of Delhi. On my request she consented to be interviewed on her poetry. To set the ball rolling, I asked, "Do you ever feel that during the creative act, you not only create but are also created, and new realities open up before you and you find yourself nearer to truth?"

Differentiating the creation of a lyric from the epical poetry, she observed, "The state of writing a lyric comes only after some intense momentum. The question of being created while creating a lyric does not arise. Such a question does arise in an epical poetry. But when it comes to singing or humming, the emotional background is already formed and any kind of truth inherent in it, gains its momentum, finds its rhythm. Thus, lyrics get created in a mental state of intense concentration. To recapitulate the mental state leading to the creation of a particular lyric would be tantamount to self-dissection which even the best surgeon cannot do. You need another surgeon for that."

Mahadevi is not only a poet, she is a painter as well. But she believes that one cannot be equally successful as a poet and a painter. In her preface to *Sāndhya-gīt* she had remarked that often a successful poet brings with him the curse of being an unsuccessful painter and *vice-versa*. But I was a bit hesitant in accepting this contention after viewing her paintings, contained in *Dīpashikhā* and *Yāmā* and that prompted me to ask her, "The paintings of *Dīpashikhā* and *Yāmā* do visualise its lyrics and the lyrics lend depth to the paintings. How did the poet as well as the painter in you escape the curse you referred to?" She elaborated on her point, "A colour denotes only one emotion and similarly a line depicts only one factual position. Thus, when an artist experienced in sketching, and good at it, starts composing a poem, only one emotion dominates, whereas a poem can be a confluence of many emotions and it becomes difficult to differentiate one from the other. Similarly, when a poet settles down to paint he is not able to depict the impact of the multi-emotional state he is in or he tries to depict it through his paining what he could not succeeded expressing fully in words.

"I do not think that either the poet or the painter in *Dipashikhā* and *Yāmā* could escape the curse. Both of them are in the bondage—all the images, all the emotions, all the colours inherent in a lyric could not find expression through the lines. The line provides only a dim background and, if seen in isolation from the poem, would appear incomplete. Similarly, if the poem is seen in isolation from the painting, it would probably appear wider, as if both the limited and the limitless are trying to merge into each other. Sometimes they succeed and sometimes they do not."

It is true that the pictorial background in the paintings lead the lyrics in *Dipashikhā* and *Yāmā* to their contextual content and, thus, facilitates their comprehension. But this costs the reader a lot, as even according to Mahadevi Varma herself 'it is not possible for the viewer to change the line-sketches as he or she desires, whereas every reader moulds the word-picture according to his own imagination.' With this in mind, I remarked that these paintings restrict the imagination of the viewer and do not allow their mind to fly freely and asked her "Don't you think that in this context, your paintings in *Dipashikhā* and *Yāmā* lend both the strength and the weakness to the comprehension of its poems?".

Contesting the suggestion implied in the question, she remarked, "The pictorial background creates a specific mental state for the reader if he reaches that level and then reads the lyrics in a detached manner. Whatever he sees as a result of the change in his mental situation, gets transformed accordingly, bringing the reader nearer the poet's perception. This is definitely an advantage as the paintings bring the mental state of the reader nearer to that of the poet, since colour and line catch the eyes and hold them on. That what meets the eyes creates an effect somewhere within. So, when he reads the lyric this effect works in his mind. He is thus bound in a way as he cannot comprehend or interpret the lyric differently. As a sad person experiences autumn even in the spring season and a happy man experiences spring inspite of the autumn around. But in this case, the reader can make no such deviation. However, if he wishes to have a free flight of comprehension just as he desires, the paintings would certainly restrict him, because they will tie him to the poet, not allowing him to comprehend the lyrics independently—not allowing him to visualise spring as autumn and *vice-versa.* It is a great boon to the poet that the reader is led to approximate his mental state, though the reader gets restricted this way. When a Sanskrit poet wrote, 'Never, never write poems for the prosaic reader,' he imagined almost a similar situation. The paintings don't permit such a situation to arise. They are, thus both bondage and freedom, at the same time."

The lyrical poetry of Mahadevi Varma is a precious treasure of the Hindi literature. Her extra-sensory experiences find spontaneous expression in these lyrics. Yet she has not attempted any epical poetry. To find out the basic reason for her indifference to this kind of poetry, I inquired, "Do you really find yourself so much fulfilled in your lyrical poetry that you do not think of writing in the mode of epical poetry. The excellent narratives found in your writings—e.g. *Smriti Ki Rekhayen* (Sketches from Memory), *Atita Ke Chalachitra* (Movies of the Past)', *Path Ke Sathi* (Co-travellers) and *Mera Parivar* (My Family)' do not permit us to believe that epical poetry does not suit your bent of mind."

Delving deep into my query, she observed, "In my prose-writing you referred to, I have recalled only those persons who came in contact with me in real life and impressed me in one way or the other. I have watched them from close quarters, identified myself with their pain as well as pleasure, giving them my whole-hearted affection. These literary creations were not even preplanned. The person happens to come across me in real life. But I don't have similar attraction for events. Searching events for epical poetry and creating characters from imagination does not suit my kind of temperament. Had these people not met me in real life, I would have perhaps looked for them in the Puranas or in the Vedic period. But general events and people I come across in life fail to sustain my interest in them when it comes to narrating them. However, the compassion that they induce in me does find expression in my lyrics and I feel relieved."

To those who find anguish and anguish alone in her lyrics, Mahadevi gave a surprise in her preface to the new edition of *Dīpashikhā*, 'I do like light, but more of the night than of the day. During the day you never find it struggling against darkness. But at night every twinkling light assumes the role of a warrior fighting a grim battle. That is why *Dīpashikhā*, the flame of a lamp, is so dear to me.' Drawing her attention to this expression I added "Yet, one is tempted to know what is it that inspires you to assess the strength of the truth struggling against untruth, light against darkness?" Weighing my questing she remarked, "One need not search outside for inspiration. Every sensitive writer, poet, artist and, I may say, even the common man, gets it from his or her environments and our environments have not yet changed. The struggle that truth has to carry out against untruth and light against darkness, has become more serious and intense now. Life has become harder and subtler. So my belief remains unshaken even today and it looks as if it will stand for a long time."

Mahadeviji once expressed a wish, in the preface of one of her anthologies: 'Just as at the dawn of my life there flowed a stream of compassion from every particle of the earth, mocking at my pleasures, I hope, an unprecedented happiness will smile from every nook and corner of the world, at the dusk of life, when after a long journey my tired being crushed under its own weight will cry out in despair and solicitation. This is how my dream goes.' Alluding to this anticipation, I asked, "Do you think, the dream you had forty years back is approaching its realisation?"

My question transported her forty years back and she observed movingly, reliving the epoch, "When I started writing, life was not like this, then I could easily have a life of comforts but I rejected that. The compassion in my life searched for itself a new field. I saw many sufferers around me and to alleviate their sufferings I took to a new path which was rather full of thorns. It was then that I dreamt, that at the successful conclusion of my journey my efforts would have brought so much happiness to others that the long journey traversed by me would not appear burdensome, as if the thorns on the way and blisters on my feet were a sort of boon to me. End of the journey has not yet come and the problems continue to persist; atmosphere is even worse, struggle is more acute. Now I have to struggle more, because the individual then did have faith, had belief and a destination too, but now he has to be told about it again and again so as to awaken him. In the circumstances, it would be difficult to say that the dream has been realised. Nobody's dreams are realised fully, but my dream is not even partially realised because, as I see, the task of awakening others has become more difficult. The age we were in did not require faith to be injected in the faithless. That age had faith all over, in us as well as in our surrounding and we had so many co-travellers. The individual finds himself all alone now and the anxiety of those who feel concerned has increased manifold. Though I admit the dream will take long to fulfil, I am not disappointed."

Bringing the discussion round to the lyrical poetry again, I raised the concluding query, "The lyric has now moved away from empirical perception and is nearing intellectualism in the garb of modernism. It takes pride in calling itself *Navgit*, following *Nayi Kavitā*. How would you react to this turning in the development of lyric?"

Reacting sharply to the present situation, Mahadevi Varma almost burst out, "In fact, there is a crisis of

Anubhūti, empirical perception, this I have been pointing out again and again. For a poet the greatest crisis is the crisis of empirical perception. Poet is not a philosopher, nor a *Smritikār* (Traditional Hindu law maker), nor a diplomat, nor a politician. In fact, he comprehends the truth of life through empirical perception and gets the perception through sensitivity. So, this is the crisis of our inner world, our emotional world, our mental world and is of such a magnitude that if not arrested, the poet will cease to be a poet. Whenever heart stops throbbing, intellect gains supremacy and the intellectualism reduces us to inaction. Intellect does not facilitate us to identify but gives us the strength of 'isms', of argumentation. Intellectualism provokes reaction in others, but emotion does not provoke another reaction; emotion identifies with another emotion. Water can merge into water, but it cannot merge with stone. They are so much different in nature that our modern poetry almost shuns emotions, leaves no room for sensitivity, no room for sentiments, rather we consider these now a poet's weakness. Our poet wants to give prominence to intellectualism and wants to sing it out, as if he sings *Chānakynīti* on the *Veena*, whereas it is neither *nīti* nor *gīta*.

"Then came the *Navgeetkārs* (New lyrists) against *Nayī Kavitā* (New Poetry), but they forget that you cannot bring every thinking close to heart just by singing it. It is only the emotions or the sentiments which can be sung. The rhythm of the flow comes with emotions only. Nobody paves the way for a stream. Stream finds its way itself. It strikes against the rocks, splashes on the stones and forms its banks. Emotions and sentiments pave their way themselves. Any kind of thinking in which we write poetry with pre-planning cannot be called a poem. You won't find poetry in that. *Navgīt* came in fact in protest against the *Nayī Kavitā*, because the *Nayī Kavitā* had turned highly intellectual, and with intellectualism it became devoid of faith which was a more serious matter. If the intellectual thinking loses faith also, it becomes worthless. It reduces itself to an intellectual exercise.

The *gita* which rose in arms against it did call itself *Navgit*, but it would be called old tomorrow. Then again some sort of new *gita* will come up. The word, *Nav* is itself relative. That which is new today will be old tomorrow. But that which will never turn old is man's emotion, his sensitivity which renews itself ever. That is why Sur's poetry never turns old, Meera's songs never turn old. Even after passing through so many ages every wave of the river Ganga remains new. Which wave of Ganga would you call old and which one new?"

(Delhi—24.3.1974)

*

Ashapurna Debi

B. 8.1.1909, Calcutta; *d.* 13.7.95; *mt.* Bengali; *car.* writing; *Awards & hons.* Līlā Puraskār, Bhubanmohinī Gold Medal, Cal. Uni., Bharatiya Jnanpith Award*, 1976, Padmashri, 1976; *Pubs. Bengali Short story collections* Shreshtha Galpa, 1953, Galpa Panchāshat, 1959, Navanīda, 1960, Sonālī Sandhyā, 1962, Jalachhabi, 1963, Kanchputī Hirā, 1967, Ek Ākāsh, Anek Tārā, 1977, *novels* Agnipriksha, 1952, Mukhar Ratri, 1961, Pratham Pratishruti*, 1964, Yuge-Yuge Prem, 1965, Subarnalatā, 1966, Bakulkathā, 1974, *complete works* Rachna Sānbhār, 3 Vols., *Hindi* (in trans.) Jīvan-Sandhyā, Pratham Pratishruti, Suvarnalata, Bakulkatha.

Truth can Never be Revealed in its Entirety

"Our history has depicted innumerable rises and falls of the past. Sometimes it chooses lamp-decor and sometimes crescendo as a medium to highlight the bright and dark lines to inspire or provoke. But it always ignores behind-the-stage changes active in the hearths and homes, different strata of society and also among the individuals themselves. Sources of human history lie in these very internal realms and not in the external events. It is a pity that the conventional history treats them as unwanted," says Ashapurna Debi, a renowned Bengali fictionist and Jnanpith Award winner, with the conviction of her heart.

Ashapurna Debi is undoubtedly a rebel, a rebel who never loses her balance. Her writings—nearing three hundred volumes in number, out of which about two hundred are novels—continually voice rebellion against the unending bonds of social traditions and customs, meaningless moral prejudices and countless atrocities on women perpetrated time and again not only by men, but also by women themselves. The trilogy of her novels—*Pratham Pratishruti*, *Subarnalatā* and *Bakulkathā*—highlights the plight of Indian woman torn apart between the do's and don'ts of society, self-contradictory concepts of the sin and the sacred imposed by selfseekers in the name of religion and the nerve-raking stresses and strains of day to day living. *Pratham Pratishruti*, the first of the trilogy, rocked the Bengali society and was widely applauded in the literary circles, winning the Tagore Award for the year. This very novel won the Jnanpith Award for 1976. The other famous novels of Ashapurna Debi are *Māyājāl*, *Agni Parikshā*, *Kakhono Din Kakhono Rāt*; her famous short-story collection *Galpa Panchāsat* deserves a special mention.

Ashapurna Debi has had no formal education, but she started writing when she was hardly thirteen. The literary and artistic atmosphere at home—her father was a painter and mother was an ardent lover of Bengali Literature—helped the talented girl to develop into a writer.

I interviewed her at her residence in Kanoongo Park in Calcutta. Her son S.K. Gupta and daughter-in-law, Nupur Gupta were present throughout the interview. The questions were addressed to her in English. S.K. Gupta rendered them into Bengali for Ashapurna Debi who replied in Bengali and Nupur Gupta provided the English translation on the spot. All the four voices were tape-recorded. This is the authentic English version of the interview.

My opening question was: "You have written many novels depicting the woman psychology in all its aspects. What was it precisely that inspired you to write the Saga of the Indian Woman in three volumes, *Pratham Pratishruti, Subarnalatā* and *Bakulkathā* covering three generations?"

She replied "From my early age I was pained to observe a difference in treatment towards women. In our society it was like that always. I wanted to find out the reason of this difference which pained me. I wanted to protest against it but I did not know how to do it. In fact, women were not given proper respect in the family and society. That was the usual picture of the society and was the order of that age. I wanted to protest in some form, a rebellion was growing inside me. There was another difficulty. We were not allowed to show our rebellious spirit. So I voiced my protest in my writings at my later age, when I had the opportunity".

I pursued further, "You had voiced this protest in your other writings also. But what was it that led you to write a series of volumes which I have just mentioned, covering three generations?"

She elucidated, "I wanted to cover three generations in their gradual state of change. In the first volume, the treatment as depicted was very miserable. I had just heard of it, I was not an eye-witness to that. The later ages I have seen myself. There were changes going on constantly at the superficial level, both socially and in private life. I felt that women were not given proper respect as they should be. I believe, there are various changes taking place from outside and there are drastic changes in the society. But in order to give proper respect and honour to the women folk many more basic changes in the society are required".

Taking up another point, I asked, "In your short stories and novels you have created many unforgettable female characters. Some people say that male writers are not able to do justice to their female characters as they portray them from the male point of view. Do you find any substance in this contention?"

She replied firmly, "I don't think so. Being a woman I would be able to create women characters better than the male writers could is not plausible. If there is a proper sense of respect, sympathy and compassion towards women in the mind of the male writer he can do as well. But there are some subtle nuances, differences of opinion and some challenges where a male writer may fail while a woman writer may depict them confidently and truthfully with her first hand experience".

Turning to her creative process, I asked, "Quoting Rabindranath Tagore, the heroine Anamika of your novel *Bakulkathā* says that a writer does not write himself, as in the creative process he is possessed by some power which dictates to him and he writes under that spell. Do you also subscribe to this belief? If so, please elaborate on this point with reference to any one of your prominent characters."

She admitted, "Yes, I very much believe in that. I begin with my own original conception and inspiration, but I find that later there are a few things being infused into my characters and, thus, I feel that the characters sometimes take new shapes and nuances which I never thought of before. I cannot disapprove of those new colours and changes. It is my belief that there is always a power working secretly behind me which instigates me to create these characters. I cannot say that in these three novels, the characters are total transcript of my imagination or I conceived them fully. It was always that the secret power worked within me and I created them as they are in these novels. But still there was a long preparation in my mind for these works. It may have been the case with other characters, but I do not readily remember them now."

Prodding her further, I asked, "In your novel *Bakulkathā* you have pointed out again and again that the type of freedom enjoyed by the modern women, like Shampa, Namita alias Rupchhanda and Rekha, was never envisaged by their grand mothers or even mothers. Don't you think that despite the right of freedom and equality attained by the modern woman, her exploitation has not yet ended? The exploitation has only changed its forms which have been sophisticated to such an extent that she herself happily falls into these male-traps as they appear to satisfy her ago. How would you react to this view?"

She replied: "Yes, your interpretation is very much correct. Women today enjoy equal footing with men and they have been given freedom which was never thought of before. But I find that the exploitation of women still continues. Women are still considered as commodity to be exploited. The society throughout the world still remains male-dominated in which women have the same kind of role to play. Offering the same kind of services, women do not receive the same kind of honour and equality. It is also a fact that women themselves are sometimes to be blamed for that. In the mind of the woman, self-respect has not yet dawned in its proper sense. She continues to remain as a doll to be placed in the hands of the male. That is the reason for the continuation of the exploitation."

Raising another point, I asked, "Your novel *Bakulkathā* is, in fact, Anamikā-Kathā, as it is not the story of Bakul as a woman. Instead, it brings out her career as a writer under the pen-name of Anamika. Anamika, the writer in Bakul, dares not write her autobiography which to her is an extremely painful process. What is your own attitude towards writing an autobiography."

She was frank in her reply, "I have often been requested to write an autobiography. But to write an autobiography, I feel one has to be very much truthful. Life is not a bed of roses; it has its painful side also. There are people who have come in my way. It is not easy and possible to depict them and, if I may add, is not proper as well. One cannot write as honestly as one should be in writing an autobiography. Private truth and social truth are different and complicated. Truth cannot be revealed in its entirety. This has to be confessed. But life is like that and there lies the reason why Anamika, the heroine of my novel *Bakulkathā* did not write her autobiography. There is the question of our environment. There are people who are connected with my life whom I cannot portray. But there is still something more. There is a thing called the essence of life which should not be misinterpreted and distorted. Therefore, I chose to reveal the truth of my life, I feel partially, in the form of my creative writings and not in the form of an autobiography."

I raised yet another point,"Your novels rouse considerable sympathy for those lovers whom society or their own circumstances did not allow to marry and instead they were married to other persons, e.g. Bakul and Nirmal of *Bakulkathā* and Suchinta and Sushovan of *Jivan Sandhyā*. But on the other hand when the girl succeeds in getting her lover finally by her indomitable will-force, the author suddenly becomes callous to them by crippling the male. In *Bakulkathā* Shampa's lover loses his limbs in a bomb explosion and Nita's lover in *Jivan-Sandhyā* loses his eyesight in an accident. Can this paradoxical attitude be traced to some obsession of the author?"

She replied "Some characters lie dormant within the mind of the creator, and some incidents do come inevitably in order to reflect those characters. In such cases, the writer is not guided by any specific attitude. If a special sympathy is shown towards any particular character then that is also bound to come quite naturally.

"I have created so many characters in my novels (about 200) and short stories (about 1000) that it is not proper, nor justified to pinpoint the attitude of the writer just by analysing a few of them. As regards the love-problems of Shampa or Nita I can say that in order to show the extreme devotion inherent in their love I have physically crippled their lovers. This was just a technical device in my writing to prove intensification and truthfulness involved in their love that surpasses the consideration of physical allurement."

Changing the topic, I asked, "You are the author of many outstanding novels. Which one of these gratified you the most or brought about a radical change in your outlook during its creation?" She replied, "In writing short stories I get full satisfaction. But since you ask me about the novels, I can say that it is *Subarnalatā* the writing of which gave me most satisfaction and sustenance. I felt a tremendous upsurge which had disturbed my mind for quite a long time. I wanted to release my thoughts, experiences and reflection of life which had haunted me for quite some time. There was the rebellious spirit in me which had gathered momentum and wanted to burst out. So in *Subarnalatā* I revealed all that I had wanted to express all these years.

"As regards the short stories, there are hundreds of them and it is difficult for me to remember them. Take for instance my story *Abhinetrī* (Actress). My own reflections towards life itself are presented in this story. Here is a woman in her various roles. Simultaneously she acts as wife, mother, daughter and in every role she tries to be successful. Women are usually born actresses and this idea forms the basis of this story."

Touching upon another issue I asked, "You must have experienced the disadvantages of being a popular writer and the price one has to pay for popularity. You must have been called upon frequently to write on demand. How do you manage to strike a balance between the quality and the quantity of your writings?"

She replied, "It is really a big problem for me. Being a popular writer I have to pay the price of popularity. But the trouble with me is that I cannot refuse any one. So I keep on meeting the constant demand which I cannot resist. But so far as quality of my writing is concerned, it is for the readers to judge."

I made another attempt, "I would like to put it this way: Are you satisfied with the writings produced by you on demand?"

She replied, "Every popular writer has to write on demand. All such writings do not give me full satisfaction always. But I shall be more sorry if I refuse to oblige those who approach me. Moreover, I do not think that all my writings are liked by all the people and are of the same quality."

Turning to the present day criticism I asked, "Do you think that the literary criticism as it stands today is of any consequence to the author or the reader? Like other writers, you might have been subjected to motivated criticism. How do you generally react to such provocations?"

She replied, "There is so far not much serious criticism of my work which I may call perverse or provocative. But if there was really any perverse criticism, I did not react much. I feel that there are differences in outlook on life and my outlook may not be accepted by all. I do not expect everyone to praise me and do not much wonder if somebody criticises me. I am fully aware of the contemporary criticism which is not honest. But as there is adulteration in other walks of life, we cannot expect much purity in the field of literary criticism also. I don't bother myself much about such criticism."

Coming to awards, I asked, "You have won many literary awards. What was your first reaction to the announcement of the Jnanpith Award on your novel *Pratham Pratishruti*? How do you view such awards as a writer? Do you think, they encourage genuine writing or just tend to foster non-literary competition?"

She replied, "My reaction to Jnanpith Award was one of surprise. I never considered myself a suitable candidate for this prestigious award. I was not prepared. How could I make it? That was the first question that came to my mind as I came to know about the announcement. As a writer I feel these awards do give a sort of encouragement to the writer and also promote her image at the highest level. It also adds to the happiness not only of the author but also of the people around her. But writing continues to proceed as one feels an upsurge in one's mind to create. Yet, it cannot be denied that awards sometimes do help in promoting the author and it also creates in her a greater sense of responsibility. But I don't think these awards have any effect on the mind of the writer as he continues writing as he feels."

Concluding the conversation I asked, "What is your concept of an author's fulfilment?" She replied, "I do not feel that any writer gets full satisfaction from any one of his writings. I always try to say what I feel and express it, but it can never be said about any literary creation that it will satisfy the author and readers in its entirety."

(Calcutta—30.9.1984)

Ismat Chughtai

B. 21.8.1915, Badayun, U.P.; *d.* 24.10.1991; *mt.* Urdu; *edn.* B.A., B.Ed.; *car.* teaching, 1939-40, Supdt., Municipal Schools, Bombay, 1941-42, writing; *Awards and hons.* Ghalib Play Award, 1975, Padmashrī, 1975; *Pubs. Urdu short story collections* Ek Bāt, 1942, Do Hāth, 1955, Choten, 1982; *novels.* Ziddī, 1942, Tedhī Lakīr, 1943, Tīn Anāḍī, 1964, Masumā, Ek Katrā-e-Khūn, 1975; *Hindi* (in trans.) *short story collection* Kunwarī; *Film Direction* Jawāb Ayegā (a film for children), a documentary on Sardar Jaffari's poems; her writings have been translated in many Indian and foreign languages.

Writing Without Inhibitions

Ismat Chughtai appeared as a challenge in the Urdu short-sotry writing—a challenge to the society as well as the contemporary story writers. Earlier, male story writers had also written several stories based on female psychology but they contained more of imagination and much less of reality. Ismat, for the first time, with her very debut in the realm of story writing, portrayed the true psyche of the middle-class Muslim girls with such fearlessness and openness that it gave the real shock of their life to the custodians of the society and religion. But Ismat continued to write with the same fearlessness and openness, uncovering the pains and torments of sisters and daughters without any dramatisation or exaggeration. No threat could deter her. Piqued by the failure, the society tried to side-track her and then resorted to taunting her for her blunt statements and when all that failed to restrict her writing, she came to be recognised as a story writer. But when her stories, such as *Lihāf* and *Chhoti Aapā*, dealing with the complexities of female psyche, stirred up the hornet's nest, even male writers started envying her.

Krishan Chandar had referred to the so-called challenge emanating from the writings of Ismat Chughtai in the Preface to his story collection, *Choten*: "Initially when Ismat's short stories appeared in the periodicals people had remarked, 'Surely, some man is writing these stories. What do our sterling women folk know about the art of story writing?' But when Ismat continued to write steadly and with determination, it was remarked, 'O forget it. What does she write...? Just trash vitriolic onslaught, always, Good God! they call it openness?' And then came a new phase: 'Yes, she's good. One of the best among women writers. Has a fine grip on female psychology, etc., etc.' And now, Ismat's name causes convulsions in male story writers. They are ashamed. Getting nervous on their own. This statement is also a manifestation of that sense of shame."

Short story is Ismat's main genre. Her creative world comprises a middle-class Muslim home where there are no farmers and labourers or capitalists or title holders. It has an aura of religiosity as well as suffocation. A veil of apartness as well as straightforwardness. There are triflings of school girls and pleasant and unpleasant frivolities of the women folk in the family. Her stories abound in the beauties and bickerings, probably more of the bickerings, which constitute a middle class home. This is just the world of our homes, neither unreal nor imaginary. This is a woman's world which has been painted and portrayed by a woman's pen in a simple language, full of similies, graphic descriptions and lively puns from everyday life.

Talking to Ismat is an experience by itself. She talks openly, without inhibitions, fabrications or exaggerations. When I met her, I found her just as I had imagined her from what I had heard about her, an open and magnanimous personality. There was a film festival going on in Bombay those days and she had a ticket for the full season. Considering that our meeting was fixed for 8-O'clock in the morning. Normally this is a busy hour for any lady but that posed no problem for her.

After a few pleasantries I straightaway came to her writing and said, "Around the time you took to writing even the male writers were viewed with some disregard and yet you, a woman, took to writing. What was that compulsion, internal or external, which made writing a necessity for you?" Staggering a bit on the word 'compulsion' she said, "There was no compulsion, neither within nor external. Writing gave me pleasure and, therefore, I started writing. My readers didn't know of my whereabouts, whether I was an urbanite or a villager. They could never guess where I was writing from. They got mad at my stories and that pleased me".

Men writers have tried to fathom female psyche as much as women writers have. But it is commonly held that, looking at women from a man's angle, they don't do justice to their female characters. Drawing her attention to this subject I tried to get her reaction. Maybe, I had failed in putting across my point correctly as she replied in anger, "Who are they to pass judgement or otherwise. I don't have to look to them for my survival." I had to repeat my question placing it in a proper perspective, "I did not mean a comment on you or your writing. I was jut referring to the common belief that men writers while portraying female characters in their stories view them from their angle and thus fail to present them correctly. Do you concur with that?" Her reply was categorical, "I have always detested that point of view and have contradicted it. They keep saying woman is like this or woman is like that, but I say a woman is just what she is made to be. In fact, men and women both turn out to be what their upbringing makes them. I did not bring up my daughters like girls, I brought them up like boys. They behave and work like boys. From the very beginning I had lived with my brother—I went ahead of girls. I kept company with boys ... I followed them wherever they went. When they played hockey, I also played hockey. Among girls, too, I made friends with advanced girls who were in service. Basically this is an economic issue. All through I worked to fend for myself. I always earned. When there was a problem I took up a job. Then I acquired training and started teaching. I was never under dictates such as, 'sit like this, move like this, go there, don't go there, talk like this, don't talk like that'. Woman has been oppressed by society, by man. She has been enslaved at the mental level. When woman ruled, she could make people see her point. Even now the working woman is respected. I fail to understand how, in a country where a woman can attain Prime-ministership, does woman get crushed? How is she burnt for the greed of dowry? We will have to look for those conditions, those circumstances, in which our Prime Minister was brought up, and create those conditions for the development of all women."

Ismat's creative canvas primarily covers the middle-class Muslim home. With the intention of probing into this secret I asked, "You have, for the first time, presented a realistic account of the psychology of Muslim women alongwith their mental and circumstantial distress and their attitude to life in your stories. What prompted you to take up such an unusual subject?" She said, "I wrote about them because they were so close to me. Those were the women around me. Among them there were some who were undergoing all types of hardships because of poverty. Among the poor, both men and women suffer because of the inadequate income. There even the man has continued to remain a slave for centuries. There neither men or women get adequate compensation for their labour. What they get is deceit, dishonesty. I felt awfully shocked at the condition of their womenfolk. I get mad when I get a shock. I felt very angry with the society and found an outlet in my stories. Thus, I used 'shock-therapy' on the society."

My next question related to the creation of her characters, "Many of the characters in your stories and novels must have come straightaway from life. You put them just as you found them in real life or they changed while you wrote them? Was there a change in your assessment of your characters as you wrote?" Referring to her creative process Ismat Chughtai explained, "No one writes with so much of analysis—the author has so much else to do. When a story is shaped, it has a bit of one woman, a bit of the other and a bit of the third one. Similarly while conceiving a male character you take a bit from one, a bit from another and a bit from yet another. The characters seldom refer to a single man or woman. A bit of the society also gets into them and that's how, like a collage, a story takes shape."

Ismat Chughtai has written an excellent story, *Chhoti Aapa*, which is also one of her favourites. It beautifully describes the spanks of love of a young Muslim girl. This story is written in the form of a diary, written by the main character, which accidentally falls into the hands of her younger sister, in the heap of old papers. The last part of the diary may serve to indicate how complicated the threads of love can be. "In such a small world of love several Shaukats, several Mehmoods, Abbases, Askaries, Yunuses and many more. 'God knows how many of them, have been placed randomly as in a shuffled pack of cards. Can someone tell which of these is the 'secret' card? Shaukat's eyes brimming with innocent tales, Mehmood's limbs which crawl like snakes, Askari's impudent hands, Yunus' sensuous lips, Abbas' lost smiles and the numerous vast chests, broad foreheads, dense hair, well-built calves, strong hands. All appear to have mingled like the threads of the yarn. Perplexed, I look at this jumble, but fail to decide which thread I should pull so that it stretches uninterrupted and with it I rise upright floating far above the skies." One may guess what ripples such a story would have caused when it was published forty years ago.

Referring to this story I asked Ismat, "Probably you did not have any *Chhoti Aapa* that you wrote this story. If you had one how would she have felt, having read it?" Reminiscing a while she said, "No, I had one *Chhoti Aapa* and a very dear one. I remember that when her husband read this story he was taken aback. He was a lovable soul. He asked me, 'Is it true? Is your *Chhoti Aapa* like that?' I said, 'Yes, exactly.' *Chhoti Aapa* got angry with me and said, 'You impertinent fool. You lie. You talk nonsense' Her husband quipped, 'No, you are so mean.' Later I told them the story had nothing to do with any single person. I had culled bits from many a woman to create my character."

With a view to knowing Ismat's attitude towards her readers I asked, "While writing do you keep the likes and dislikes of you reader in mind or all your attention is engaged in expressing your feelings and you go on writing under some spell?" She replied, "I never found it necessary to know whether the readers liked my writings or not. I never wrote with the intention of pleasing the readers. After the publication of my first few stories there was such a demand for my writings that I never had time to think of all that."

To provoke her somewhat, I enquired, "Which was your first story and what was people's reaction to it?" She said, "The title of my first story was *Genda* (calendula flower). It was a very short piece, somewhat unique. Genda is the name of the girl in that story. A rich boy beguiles her and she becomes pregnant. This is quite common among the poor. There were objections and objections against that story."

Lihaaf is the most controversial story written by Ismat which created violent ripples in the society. This story has been presented in the form of the reminiscences of small girl whose mother, while going out of town for a few days, leaves her with a friend. This friend is the *begum* (young wife) of an old *nawab* (wealthy landlord). But since the *nawab* keeps busy with the young and fair boys he is fostering, his poor *begum* is languishing in neglect. But soon she develops intimacy with a maid and finds an egress to happy living. At night the girl's bed is placed in *begum's* room but she cannot sleep because of the fright, and almost dies of fear looking at the jumpy elephant-like shadow of *begum's lihaf* (quilt) on the wall. She very innocently describes that frightful night in her reminiscence: "When I softly went and peeped into the bed-room, I saw *begum's* maid-servant Rabbo massaging her body entwined round her waist. 'Take off your shoes' she said to me scratching her ribs ... and I quietly slipped into my quilt. Surr, surr phut ... kutch-*begum's* quilt was flapping in the dark like an elephant. 'Oh, God ...' I let out a hushed sound. The elephant jumped in the quilt and settled down. I too became quiet. The elephant rolled again. I got chilled to the bone. Then I decided to have courage and light up the bulb just above me. The elephant was stirring itself, as if it was struggling to sit on its hind legs. There were sounds of slurping as if it was licking some savoury sauce. And then I got it. *Begum sahiba* had not taken any food today and the wretched Rabbo, greedy as she is, must be devouring some delicious snack. I widened my nostrils and took deep breath to smell the air. But didn't get anything except the fragrance of scents, sandal and henna. The quilt started ballooning once again. I tried hard to lie quiet but the quilt started making such strange forms that I shuddered. It looked as if a frog was swelling and with a croak was about to jump on me, 'Mm ... Mother!' I took courage to say softy. But it went unheard. The quilt kept acquiring all sorts of forms in my imagination. Scared all the while I stepped out on the other side of my bed and groping for the switch, I pressed it. The elephant tumbled under the quilt and flattened. In that acrobatics a part of that quilt opened up and—my God! I darted back into my bed."

One can guess what a hue and cry this story would have engendered about fortyfive years ago, though it just strives to emphasise that even a noble bride may get compelled to find escape-routes when so completely neglected by her husband. Bringing in the reference of that story I asked, "Your stories must have literally stirred the hornet's nest, those days. Your unbeaten subjects and open descriptions must have created a storm. They must have shocked the custodians of society to death and, in turn, they would have cast all possible aspersions against you. Please tell us something about those reactions."

Recalling the bygone days she said, "Those stories did raise a lot of hue and cry but I did not get to know the people's reaction correctly. People's letters were received at the office of the journals and they were not considered fit enough to be redirected to me. The editor of *Saqui*,Shahid Ali Dehalvi was like my elder brother. He was of the view that those vulgar letters should not reach me. He kept me completely out of their reach.

"It was much later that I got to know of such letters. I got to know of all that hue and cry when one day I got summons from the court. That gave me a hearty laugh. The suit was 'King George Fifth vs. Ismat Chughtai'. It amused me to think that the 'great' king should have read my story so that he had filed a suit against me. Now I can laugh it away but then it had made me angry as well. The case went on for three-four years, until around 1944-45. Later I got to know that a Delhi-based publisher had some enmity with that publisher in Lahore. He had filed the suit with a view to thwarting the sale of my book. But it worked the opposite way and proved profitable to me. The book came into great demand and the edition sold like hot-cakes. Then the demand for my stories shot up and I earned lots of money."

Referring to many of her characters I asked Ismat, "Do you keep a tight grip over your characters from the beginning to the end or leave them on their own as they grow?" She replied rather authoritatively, "I keep my characters under my control. I decide where I want to take them and usher them in accordingly; I won't let them lose way or deviate. I may kill them or let them live at will. There I hold the status of God. I am free to do what I like. I feel awfully strong, then."

To elicit her reactions to the modern short story I asked, "You will have noticed the change the modern short story has gone through. Earlier the story found its base in events and the development of its characters. But, now the stories based on events and characterisation are considered inferior. What is your opinion in this regard?" Ismat's reaction was sharp: "I pay no heed to what others say and don't care for what they say. They may be right but I am also right. They have their own experiences, I have mine. I have never ever objected to anything. Earlier, when I lived under all sorts of constraints and my ways were vehemently criticised, I had not cared about anything; nor do I care, now."

This reply reminded me of Krishan Chandar's comment on her stories: "I feel extremely happy when people abuse Ismat Chughtai because, then, they abuse themselves, they abuse their own filth which they want to camouflage under the garb of some scent they call spirituality, they abuse this ghost which Ismat has exposed time and again in her stories—which the society wants to preserve under the dark folds of its false civility and religiosity. Ismat has very frequently exposed this fraud and hypocricy of the society in a sharp satirical tone which cuts deep like a sharp dagger."

(Bombay—4.1.1984)

*

I. Saraswati Devi

B. 1918, Narasapur, Distt. West Godavari, Andhra Pradesh; *mt.* Telugu; *car.* Social work and writing; *Awards and hon.* MLA for eight years in A.P. Assembly, Sahitya Akademi Award*, 1983; *Pubs. Telugu short story collection* Swarnakamalālu*, *novels* Darijerinā Prānulu, Jivita Valayalu, Vyjayanti, Bhavati Bhiksham Dehi, Anupamā, Jivita Patham.

Multi-Dimensional Sensibilities

Saraswati Devi has a prominent place among those women writers who have enriched Telugu fiction during the past four-five decades. Her fiction is known for its close-knit structure with a clear beginning, a gripping plot and suggestive ending. Her short stories evince psychological insights into the complexities of the human mind. Her award-winning book *Swarna Kamalalu* presents a variety of short stories depicting mainly the urban middle class, its pains and pleasures, hopes and disappointments, economic tribulations and conditioned attitudes towards life. Her novels show concern for the downtrodden and aim at their social and economic uplift. She believes in the all-round awareness of the writer and his concern for the fellow beings. He is not to be an intellectual elite working in isolation.

I met her at Hyderabad during a lecture tour of the southern universities and found myself in conversation with her about her writings. Opening the discussion, I asked, "You must have drawn many characters of your short stories and novels from the real life. Did you ever feel that your assessment of them in the real life underwent a sea change during the creative act?"

She thought for a while, recapitulating her characters, and replied, "The characters in my stories are created by imagination. Incidents have been picked up from real life. The characters have been adapted to suit situations. For example, in my story '*How Much is the Value of a Smile*', I have shown that a wife prefers to keep her husband happy and see him smile over everything else in her life. They love each other intensely. But the poverty and his bad habit lead him to debts and he attempts to put an end to his life. His wife saves him from suicide, secures the required amount and goes to his office to repay the debts. He feels sorry, sympathises with her for her innocent and sincere efforts to save their family and walks up to Husain Sagar tank. By that time, the area was heavily guarded by security police as some person had committed suicide by jumping into the tank and the dead-body was brought out. Here the heroine of the story comes running to the spot, she mistakes the dead-body for her husband's and jumps into the tank to put an end to her life. It is now the turn of her husband to lament and weep over her dead-body. Why had she been running about to get money, pay it in his office and prevent his death? Her only aspiration in her life was to see him smile happily. But what was the price she had to pay for? Already, a mother of five children and pregnant for the sixth time, her poverty does not come in the way of her love for her husband—a lofty sentiment of a wife is expressed to appeal to the hearts of the readers. The Family Planning Section of AIR had asked for a short story. Yet the depiction of human element is not lost even in this propaganda story.

"Another story was about an army with its Captain stationed in an isolated building. They were spending their time merrily. One morning they found a baby wrapped up in old clothes thrown about. Many of the soldiers went their way casually but two of them lifted up the child and took him inside the tent. They feed the boy with milk and go in search of a wet nurse to feed the baby. They got one and decided to protect her. The wet nurse was feeding the baby when their Captain throws lustful glances at her. The soldier who witnessed this immediately fired his gun at the Captain, forgetting the consequences. Here, I wanted to depict the merciful hearts of the otherwise tough-minded soldiers towards a tender baby, but they could not bear someone's best interfering in the care of the child. Hard-headed as the soldiers are—they have a soft corner too. The title of the story is "*Humanism Awakened—Passions Aroused*".

To find out how she makes a choice of the form to write in, I inquired, "How do you determine the form of your writings? Did it ever happen that you started writing a short story, but the vast potential of the theme compelled you to give it the form of a novel?" She replied, "The art of short story is different. It is a snap shot; you have to show the entire world in a miniature picture. A short story has to be planned as a short story. It requires only one incident. A novel requires a life span. The writer has to lay down his fundamental theories and has to justify them through the life. Even though, it will be lengthy the novelist has to give the contemporary historical background to the novel. The skill for writing a novel is different from that of a story. From the technical point of view, one should not try to write a novel out of a story, or summarise a novel into a story because the fundamental structure is different. Many authors who have made such attempts have failed miserably. I believe in differentiating between the two different techniques".

Knowing her interest in the reader, I asked, "Do you have readers in mind at the time of writing or you concentrate mainly on expressing yourself?" She replied, "When I write, I keep in mind human psychology and motivations. My ideas do not arouse my readers for any action. My writings are meant to make people reflect—to give a soothing touch to their perturbed minds. I want to touch their hearts. I do not present my thoughts first as they come to my mind. I would refine them, beautify them and skilfully present them and make every effort to see that they appeal to the hearts. I am not a sensational writer, creating unrest in the minds of the readers. I want people not to think with their head but feel within their hearts. I try all methods to move the hearts. My writings are for readers with whole-heartedness".

Referring to her female characters, I asked, "You have portrayed both male and female characters in your short stories and novels. Some people say that only women writers can do justice to the female characters, whereas male writers only project their one-sided view point. What is your experience in this respect?" She replied, "I make no distinction between men and women. My writings also do not have any leanings. I have not written to abuse male domination nor have I appealed for special treatment to women. They belong to one unit and are meant to live together. They have separate characteristic behaviour. Consciously, I have not shown any partiality to either side. I have depicted life only as it is found in reality. I believe that writer should be above prejudices and partialities. His goal is to aim at higher sentiments".

Trying to find out her own favourite short stories, I asked, "Could you enumerate some of your short stories which gave you sense of fulfilment and which you consider your best?" She began hesitatingly, "I like all my stories. But of them, I remember the story about a man unaffected by the darkness of life and the one entitled "*Laughing Man*". The first story depicts a man unmoved as the mountain in the face of successive problems. He writes wishing well for the entire society and his personal hardships do not make him feel bitter or revengeful. He is high above the worldly pains and pleasures and prays for the happiness of the society around him. The second story is about a young man with all natural desires and aspirations. He cannot satisfy any of them and faces odds and feels frustrated. He has learnt to laugh among his problems and is a merry man who understands the futility of efforts for satisfaction of his ambitions. The smile on his lips gives the impression that his thoughts are beyond life as if he has conquered his desires and is sublime. The radiant smile on his lips is ever present. I have written many such stories. They have gone deep into spiritualism and many people have appreciated them".

My next question was "Could you name any writer who inspired you the most?" She replied, "I appreciate all writings that can arouse emotion and feeling. I like such authors of any language. I started writing at the age of sixteen when no one influenced me. All my reading came later whatever I read, my writing came out of my own mind.

Coming to the need for translations of masterpieces of one language into another, I observed, "Literature can and does unite people, whereas politics tends to divide them. But language and script pose a big problem by confining its appeal to only those who know them. What would you suggest to enhance the appeal of literature beyond these barriers?" She replied, "Writings should have a universal outlook. Man is man, to whatever language or country he may belong. It is literature that can bring together men of all languages, races and cultures. We can have world peace only by such unity. But when writers are interested only in the progress of their own region-language or section we will be creating more differences. We can say that even harm is possible through such writings. Society will be misguided by such people. This can be achieved by translations in as many languages as possible".

(Hyderabad—25.2.1984)

*

Amrita Pritam

B. 31.8.1919, Gujranwala (now in Pakistan); *mt.* Panjabi; *car.* writing; *Awards and hons.* Sahitya Akademi Award*, 1956, Bharatiya Jnanpith Award*, 1981, Member Parliament, Rajya Sabha (nominated), 1986-92, D. Litt. (hon. cau.), Delhi Uni.; *Pubs. Punjabi poetry* Sunehre, 1955, Kasturī, 1959, Nāgmani, 1964, Kāgaz te Kainvas*, 1973, Mein Jamā Tu, 1977, *short story collections.* Panj Vareh Lambī Sadak, Ik Shahar Dī Maut, 1971, Hīre Dī Kanī, 1977, Tīsari Aurat, 1978; *novels* Doctor Dev, 1949, Pinjar, 1950, Band Darwāzā, 1961, Ik Sī Anitā, 1964, Chak No. 36, 1964, Jalāvatan, 1970, Yātrī, 1971, Uninjā Din, 1979, Tehrawān Sūraj, 1979, Kore Kāgaz, 1982, Nā Rukmani Nā Rādhā, 1985; *misc.* Safarnāmā, 1976, Ik Udās Kitāb, 1976, Muhabbatnāmā, 1980, Shauk Surahī, 1981, Kadī Dhup Dā Safar, 1982, Akshar Kundalī, 1988; *autobiography,* Rasidi Tikat, 1976; widely translated in various Indian and foreign languages; Hindi translation of almost all works available.

Flights of the 'I' in Me

Amrita Pritam's life and writings are a little removed from the usual beaten path of ordinary mortals. Both contain a rejection of tradition and a passionate search for individual truth. That is why perhaps both are full of a sense of daring and have remained a question mark in the public eye. Amrita's creative talent has not been limited to any genre—hers is a versatile genius. Basically a poet, she has made a valuable contribution to other genres as well. Whether a poem or a novel, a story or an essay—woman's anguish and her pitiable condition in a male-dominated society are brought to the fore. But the underlying theme of Amrita's writings is the pulse of life, not an escape from or indifference to it. Facing life in all its complexity with all one's strength—not caring even for the risks involved or the outcome—is the main motif of her writings. Despite her anger with the basic injustices of life, her writings overflow with love for entire humanity.

Meeting Amrita is an experience to be enjoyed. A man brought up in a conservative traditional manner is in for a shock on first meeting her, but it is soon lost in the poetic mood that her personality creates in the viewer. As far as the eye can see—art and poetry find expression on the walls, the almirah-doors, the lamp-shades—every bit of the living room. One must know Gurmukhi and Persian scripts to fully enjoy this atmosphere because many of her own moving poems and those of her favourite poets are inscribed in them. Life size paintings on the walls add to the artistic clan.

Recovering from this magic spell when I expressed my wish to discuss her writings with her, she readily agreed on one condition. She said, "Ask whatever you want to. I will reply to all your questions and doubts in writing." She explained that when she sits down to write, paper becomes for her some kind of a mirror which reflects her inner soul and helps her confront her own self.

Amrita Pritam's characters come from all walks of life and are seen as multi-faceted and conflicting personalities. Their reactions to others as well as to their own selves, are at times simple and, at times, complex. My first question was, therefore, related to her characters, "After reading your narratives and autobiography *Raseedi Tikat*, one feels that many events and acquaintances in your life have found expression in your writings. In the course of writing a story or a novel have you ever felt that the pre-conceived notions about people's actions and reactions are beginning to fade away and instead new and deeper meanings beginning to emerge, taking you closer to their truth and reality? If so, please enlighten us on this miraculous ability of the creative process in the context of any of your novels or characters."

Getting the point of my question she said, "The transfigurations of the creative process cannot be expressed in words. I can only say that this creative process has the divine ability to infuse life into forms of clay and these imaginary characters become so real and life-like that the author feels he can recognise them if they ever chance to come his way. Many readers make inquiries about certain characters.

"*Ninā* was the main character of my novel *Ghonslā*. She was a product of my imagination. But she became so real that one night she asked me in my dream why I had turned her life into a tragedy. She wanted to live. The hero of the novel *Yātri* was based on a real person. I had seen him as a child. I had imagined him growing up but had not seen him in his youth. Years after the novel had been published I happened to meet him. He was so ordinary and so simple that there was no possible likeness between him and the hero of my novel. It seemed as if the final truth lay in the art that created him in my novel and not in the ordinary person that he was. *Doctor Dev* was a figment of my imagination. But years later when I met someone I thought I had created the character earlier and only met him much later.

"Some characters are too powerful to be fully pinned down in words. Their power is beyond the reach of words. The beauty of some characters goes far beyond the limited confines of reality which always lags behind."

My next question concerned the reader, "While writing do you think only of expression your innermost feelings or of the readers too who you want to reach out to?" Her reply was unambiguous, "While writing I think of no other reader than myself. At that moment I am the sole reader of my writing, the only spectator of my 'self'."

To find out how Amrita decides the genre for her writings I said, "You have written stories, novels and essays and they have all been talked about. Still I feel that you are basically a poet. Most of your novels and stories are poetic. Is it that sometimes you have found the poetic impulse taking the form of a novel or a story?"

Talking about the themes of her writings she said, "Idea is important in my *nazma*, not the form of expression. I do not interfere with the form, it takes on its own. Many a time have I seen a poem turning into a story and a story sometimes encompasses so much of the world within its short stride that it becomes a novel. Sometimes a projected novel seems of its own to reach up to the sky and then return to me in the shape of a *nazma*."

Much has been said on the role and utility of literature in life. Many intellectuals have gone to the extent of saying that to look for any utility in literature is being unfair to both literature and litterateurs. To elicit her view on the subject, I said, "You have poured your experiences and your soul's anguish in your writings and made them everyone's. That is why the reader can so easily identify himself with it. In your poems he hears his own anguish and his spirit is calmed. From this point of view do you see any usefulness of literature?" She said, "In my opinion, literature's usefulness does not lie in the banner you hold or the slogan you shout. It is like the fragrance of a flower which is both inside the flower and outside it."

In her poem *Takhliqi Amal* (Creative Process) Amrita Pritam has compared a *nazma* to the abortion attempted by an unmarried girl: "An unmarried girl's abortion is perhaps the same." Taking the simile further I said,"Besides being a writer, you are a mother too. This prompts me to know if you don't find any similarity between the birth-pangs of a mother and the creative process of an author. After the delivery the mother feels the same relief and the same sense of joy at seeing the child as the poet does after the creation of a poem. The comparison you have drawn seems, however, to suggest the presence of shame and remorse."

Elucidating it further, Amrita Said, "This is both the agony and the ecstasy at one and the same time but not the remorse at all. It refers to that awareness of experience which steps out of the familiar threshold of traditional ethical bonds and is then surprised at itself."

In her stories and novels Amrita has held the narrow selfishness of man and society responsible for all the problems of woman though in her book *Nārī: Ek Drishtikon* (Woman: A Viewpoint) she has herself admitted that more that anyone else women themselves obstruct the path of woman's liberation and development. Right-thinking men like Sajjad, Sahir, Imroz and her husband in Amrita's own life, the father of the hero of *Yātrī*, Sanjay of *Terahanvān Sooraj* and Karim of *Uninjā Din* are after all part of this very world, even if a few in number. Focussing the discussion on this point I said, "Man and Woman are complementary, neither of them is self-sufficient. That is why perhaps our ancient sages had developed the concept of the *Ardhanārīsvar*. Won't it amount to some kind of female-chauvinism if we blame man for all woman's problems?"

It was a loaded question, bound to evoke a strong response. Amrita was full of anger. "In the philosophy of the *Ardha-nārīsvar*, both the parts of God are complementary to each other. How is it then that one part of God became the ruler and the other merely the ruled? In the background are those negative forces which worship God only in name and not in spirit."

In many of Amrita's books available in Hindi no details of the translator or translation are given. The reader may even think that Amrita wrote them in Hindi. Examples of this omission can be sighted in *Kadi Dhoop Kā Safar* and *Voh Admi, Voh Aurat* published by Rajpal and Sons, *Jalāvatan* by the Hind Pocket Books and the three collections—one of her eight favourite novels, one of select short stories and one of essays—all published by the Bharatiya Jnanpith. Drawing her attention to this misleading situation I said, "Were all your works, now available in Hindi, translated from the original Punjabi or written directly in Hindi?" She clarified, "I write my essays in Hindi but all other writings are translations from Punjabi."

Amrita has tried to make her meaning clear at the end of her novels like *Yātri*, *Terahanvān Sooraj* etc. by adding a postscript. Referring to that I said, "Were you so uncertain of your readers' understanding that you thought it necessary to add a statement at the end of your novels? I feel that when a writer offers an explanation outside of her works, she is more of a reader than a writer. In that case it would not be fair to consider it as the only and final statement. That is why perhaps D.H. Lawrence had said, 'Trust the tale, not the teller.' " Justifying her explanatory notes she said, "Many a time talking of the creative process is part of the creative process itself. It is not born of any mistrust of the readers' ability. A point comes when one can say, 'Trust the tale and the teller too".

I now focussed on Amrita Pritam's *Raseedi Ticket*. In one's enthusiasm to live life one can face with fortitude inner and outer hurts. But while writing one's autobiography, one has to relive the pain and that too with a cool head which is relatively more difficult. I, therefore, said, "Overcoming all the risks of writing an autobiography, the frankness with which you have written *Raseedi Ticket* shows that living one's life one's own way is less challenging than writing about it in one's autobiography.

Did you feel the same way?" She replied serenely, "When outspokenness is valued for its own sake, then it is very difficult to come to terms with it. But when it is a reflection of one's inner state of mind, then it does not have to borrow anything from bravely-contrived words".

Going through *Raseedi Ticket* one feels that despite leading a life full of ups and downs Amrita Pritam has been lucky in always having her people by her side because usually the betrayal comes from one's own people. From this point of view, more than Sahir, Sajjad and Imroz her two children deserve full credit. The intensity of mental agony they went through while siding with their mother can be gauged from the question her son posed regarding her relationship with Sahir. Touching upon this delicate matter I said, "Looking at your life I think that more than Sajjad, Sahir, Imroz and your children, your husband deserves credit for ignoring the social ostracisation and letting you lead your own life. As one learns from your autobiography, he accepted his loneliness without a murmur and without a complaint to anyone. Do your ever think of him in this light?"

Amrita's reply to this rather very personal question (posed in the context of her writings) was so convoluted that it was difficult to fathom its true meaning. "Those were the riches of mine 'I' ". This confession is the key to her life and her writings.

The rather strange court room scene in *Yah Sach Thā* and the vision the hero Sanjay has of hell and heaven with the heroine Geeta in the middle seem symbolic of the juxtaposition of sentience and oblivion. Amrita has also mentioned a few sessions she has had with a psychiatrist in *Raseedi Ticket*. Reminding her of them I said, "Are those scenes based on the sessions with the psychiatrist you have referred to in your autobiography?" Her reply was again swift and unambiguous, "No. I had had some sessions with a psychiatrist way back in 1961—the time I had written most of *Kālā Gulāb*. My later writings have not been influenced by these sessions."

My next question related to the interaction between life and literary creativity, "In the context of any of your works can you say that intellectually and mentally you did not remain what you were after writing it? I feel that the author alone does not create his works, his works also create him and he is not even aware of it." Conceding the mutual interdependence of an author and his writings she said, "Yes, I do agree that writings also make an author. I have been aware of it after each of my creations was finished."

Going through the already published works the author often feels that had the work been written differently, it would have created a better impact. A few writers make the required alterations in the next edition while some others use those ideas in the next work. Referring to this I said, "Have you ever tried to improve your writings in their later editions? If so, kindly tell us which work or character or instance you have altered and in what way."

She said, "I can mention here some portions of *Raseedi Ticket* which when published first seemed fantasies of my imagination. I felt that they had no groundwork of reality. I deleted these portions in the second edition and gave reasons for doing so. These portions related to my children's marriage".

Every writer faces some problem or the other at the hands of his contemporaries. To know Amrita's attitude towards her critics I said "You must have had varied experience with your critics and readers. Don't you think that if instead of the present day motivated criticism the writer gets the reactions of his discerning readers, the possibilities of his writing getting the right direction grow stronger?"

Going into the depths of the question she said, "I agree that the relationship between the writer and the reader is the only true relationship. The writer is also a critic because his writings are a criticism of life, criticism of the reality of life in relation to the author's vision of life, criticism of the limitations of life in relation to the immense possibilities of life. But the writer's vision is the outcome of his constant ocean-churning. He has the intensity of feelings, depth of thinking and a style of writing. More than all this, he is entitled to offer his criticism because he is deeply in love with life. If all these qualities can be found in the critics commenting on the author's creative criticism of life, it would be wonderful. It would then, form a bridge between the writer and the reader. But it does not happen that way. The critic does not usually possess these traits. He, therefore, ends up spoiling the relation between the writer and the reader".

My last question pertained to the evergrowing craze and competition for literary awards: "What was your immediate reaction to the announcement of the Bhāratīya Jñānpīth Award? Do such awards really promote genuine writing or encourage only extra-literary manipulations?" Amrita's reply was categorical, "The immediate reaction was of freedom from economic pressures with the great consolation that this came my way without my having to belittle myself in my own eyes. In my opinion money, power and fame are very precious weapons which can help chisel and materialise many dreams. The only condition is that the hands handling them act with dignity and discretion. When the hands prove weaker and smaller, these weapons can be suicidal."

(New Delhi—12.2.1984)

*

Popati Hiranandani

B. 17.9.1924, Hyderabad Sindh (now in Pakistan); *mt.* Sindhi; *edn.* B.A. (B.H.U); *car.* teaching, Former Head, Sindhi Deptt., K.C. College, Bombay; *Awards & hons.* All India Sindhi Boli Aur Sahitya Sabha Award, 1962, Min. of Education and Culture Award, 1978, Sahitya Akademi Award*, 1982; *Pubs. Sindhi short story* Rangīn Zamāne Jun Ghamghīn Kahānyān, 1953, Kali Gulāb ji Sagharu Sharāb jo, 1967, Moon Tokhe Pyār Kyo, 1975, Khizān Jo Dauru Pūro Thiyo, 1976, Shāhnāz, 1983, Kafan Dhakī Zindagī, 1985; *novels.* Manju, 1953, Hasiratun-ji-Turbat, 1961, Jia mein Jhurī Tan mein Tatī, 1966, Sailabu Zindagī a Jo, 1980; *lit. crit.* Azīm Shakhsu ain Alim Shah,: Sindhī Tahzīb Jo Rūhu, 1983, Sindhi Shairanji Hindī a mein Kavitā, Tankidi Mazmūn; *autobiography* Muhinji a Hayati a ja Sonā-Rūpā Varqa*, 1980; English Sindhis—The Scattered Treasure, 1980, History of Sindhi Literature: Post-Independence, 1984, The Coward (a collection of short stories, in trans.), 1987, I belong to a Land (poems), 1991.

The Woman Needs Awareness More Than Freedom

Popati Hiranandani was born in Hyderabad Sind in the Hyderabadi Amil clan of Sind. Her forefathers were Diwans under the Muslim kings. When Popati's father expired, she was only ten years old. The mother had to play the role of both father and mother to her seven small children. Popati, being the second eldest child, had to earn when she was only fourteen. Her father had wanted the bold and courageous Popati to ensure that her younger sisters and brothers studied up to graduation at least. He also wanted her to learn Sanskrit. Popati had cleared her matriculation with Persian as her compulsory second language, so she decided to learn Sanskrit and enrolled herself with the Banaras Hindu University as a casual student. Thus she started earning and learning and obtained her B.A., with distinction in Sanskrit.

From her young age, Popati felt that woman in our society had to face many odds and suffer innumerable miseries. Hence she took her pen to try to bring some awareness among women. Her bold and fearless expressions frightened all her friends and relatives and some of them would openly say, "Who will marry this terribly frank girl?" But Popati was not at all concerned about these remarks. She made her way through the literary world with her articles and essays. Gradually she tried her hand at other genres also. She wrote plays, stories, novels and poems. Her publications include six collections of short stories, four novels, six collections of essays and two books of literary criticism. Her stories have been translated into English, Hindi, Gujarati, Marathi, Malayalam, Telugu and Tamil.

I met Popati Hiranandani during my recent visit to Bombay. In the course of our discussion I said, "You have created many characters in your stories and novels. Do these characters come directly from life around you or undergo a change during the creative process?"

Searching within, she replied, "Yes, it is true that my characters come directly from life. This is also true that when I start writing, I do have some faint ideas about the characters in mind which change as I proceed. Sometimes these changes are minor, at others major and quite startling. Sometimes the characters turn out to be entirely different from how I had initially conceived them. With experience and maturity I myself like to recast some of my characters. For example, in one of my novels *Hasiratun-ji-Turbat* (The Graveyard of my Unfulfilled Desires) I had depicted a lady who fell in love with her step-son. If I were to re-write this novel it won't be the step-son but somebody else. I would still like to depict the lady rebelling against the society which compelled her to accept an old man as her husband, but in a different way. Similarly, in *Jia-mein-jhoori-Tan-Mein-Tāti* (The Yearning of my Heart and the Craving of my Body) I have depicted a girl who waits for her lover for six long years to return to her. He had gone abroad and married her friend in London. But this girl waits for the return of her beloved and when he does return, she is glad to have him back to herself. If I were to rewrite this novel, I would make the girl shut her door on the man who deserted her and ruined her golden youth. When I wrote these novels, I was not mature enough.

"When I was young, I used to think that all the social evils were due to the wrong behaviour and wrong ideas of the male members of the society. Therefore, almost all my stories relate to the injustice done to women by men. But now I know that at least fifty per cent of the social evils are due to the evil-minded or foolish women. These women create situations in which men are compelled to misbehave with other women, that is, their wives, mothers and sisters.

"In this way, as far as the writer is concerned, religion, society politics etc. acquire new meanings and dimensions with the change of time and advancement of his or her age because experience and observation bring maturity of thought. Therefore, many of my stories written long long ago seem to me 'not so good' now.

"But there are some stories which though written about twenty or thirty years ago are as relevant today as they were then. For example, *Khuwāb* (Dream) was written in 1949. It is about a man who loses his wife in his old age. He had married her when she was only eleven. With her dead body lying before him, he recalls all the joys of his youth, her radiant smile and his own passion for her, her shyness and his romantic approaches, the conjugal bliss and the amorous pleasures that engulfed them both and the tenderness of the shared love between them. These descriptions and glimpses of life are as true today as they were then. Hence the story is fresh even today.

"Similarly, the characters and the situations in *Brahmā-jī-Bhūla* (Brahma's Blunder) are true even today. In fact, there are a number of stories which I wouldn't want to change because their import and message, convictions and values, are eternal. They don't change."

I probed further, "You have written short stories as well as novels, plays as well as essays. How do you determine the form of your writing? Did it ever happen that you started with one form, but it did not make much headway and then you had to drop it and start afresh?"

She thought for a while and said, "I started with writing essays, though from my childhood I had longed to be a poet. But Sind was a Muslim dominated state. There were so many restrictions on a Hindu girl's movements. One such restriction was that a Hindu girl would not sit with a male, (be he a poet or a writer) and learn from him the technique of composing a poem. (Hence, even now you cannot find a Sindhi poetess in the real sense of the term). In those days Sindhi poetry was composed according to the technique of Persian prosody and in order to learn the rules of the Persian prosody we had to learn *Vazan*, Bahar, *Kafiya*, *Radeef* etc. from somebody who could explain these terms. Being forbidden to learn these things from a poet, I had to satisfy myself with writing poetic-prose which did not require any technique. These writings of mine were greatly appreciated by the common man in Sind because the technically perfect Sindhi poem could only be understood by the learned few. Afterwards, I translated a few stories from Hindi into Sindhi and only then did I attempt to write a short story in original Sindhi.

She added, "I wrote plays for my school functions. The Hindus in Sind wanted their children to know something about their own religion. So in order to satisfy them the teachers (I was also a school teacher) had to present plays which mirrored the Hindu doctrines or mythological characters. I wrote *The Coronation of Chhatrapati Shivaji*, *Rana Pratap*—The Uncrowned King of Chittore and *Shakuntalā* (based on Kalidasa's work). Hyderabad was a small town. The whole town used to turn up at the entertainment programmes arranged by the school authorities. People greatly applauded the performance of the girls. Parents of all the school girls started calling me *Guruji*!

"Encouraged by their appreciation and admiration and to satisfy my urge to write poetry, I wrote a play entitled *Zebunnisā* and rendered some couplets of Aurangzeb's daughter in Sindhi. The girls were simply thrilled by the costumes and scenes of the Moghul-palace. But partition of the country was declared by that time and the Muslim Collector of Hyderabad Sindh banned the staging of that play! The poetess in me was terribly hurt at this order of the Collector, because my Zebunnisa had not been allowed to recite her couplets.

"After the partition, I worked as a teacher in Sind Model High School, Bombay. The Principal of the school was a great devotee of Lord Krishna. So I wrote the plays entitled *Sudāmā*, *Subhadrā*, *Sant Surdās*, *Satyabhāma* etc. for the school-functions. Long after I had left that school and joined college as a Professor, I wrote *Assanjo*

Vajoodu (our Existence in India). It is about the struggle of the Sindhis for the preservation of their distinct identity in India. This play of mine won the first prize in a competition organised by the Rajasthan Sindhi—Sahitya Akademi. I composed ballads also for college-programmes. I write short stories but the poetic-prose form comes directly from my heart. Sometimes I start writing an article in prose but it changes itself into poetic-prose. It happened with *Jadahn-moon-Khuhindo-Pahiriyo* (When I have Worn the Pink-dress of Marriage) *Alvidah! Oh Sacha* (Farewell! Oh truth! I bid adieu to you!) and *Muhinjo-Janama-Ute-Thiyo-Ahe* (I am Born in this Place)".

Drawing her attention to the role of the reader, I said, "Do you think of your readers while writing or just of your own ideas and thoughts?" She replied frankly, "I think about the readers only when I write for some popular newspaper. Otherwise I only want to pour out my feelings and thoughts. While writing I never hesitate or stop. I am very frank, rather blunt. I don't try to restrict myself or impose any limitations when I pour out myself. Once the Principal of my school summoned me and said, 'Do not write such articles as may frighten away the orthodox class of our community.' But when I explained to him that if we, the educated girls, did not try to awaken the members of our society, who else would do so? He did not say a word. In the heart of his hearts, he agreed with my way of thinking".

Then I enquired about her women-characters. I said, "Men-writers as well as women-writers depict women characters. Some critics are of the opinion that men cannot do justice to women because men judge a woman from their male-angle. It is also said that woman is the greatest enemy of woman. In *Brahmā-jī-bhūla* (Brahma's Blunder) even you have said that a woman is a strange creature. She cannot bear to see or praise the virtue of another woman, she will take a magnifying glass and magnify the defect.' Your story *Diary* also depicts a heroine who fails to understand her own close friend.

How will you react to these contradictory remarks of the critics? Do you think that a woman- writer does full justice to her female character?"

Popati Hiranandani said, "It is true that a male-writer cannot fully understand a woman. Hence he cannot do full justice to his women-characters because he measures a woman from a man's angle only. It is also true that woman is the greatest enemy of woman, the reason being that a woman's life has not been allowed to develop. If a daughter-in-law is tortured by her mother-in-law, she in turn should not trouble her own daughter-in-law when she herself becomes the mother-in-law. But this doesn't happen. She repeats the behaviour she had received from her mother-in-law.

"You have referred to 'Brahma's Blunder' and 'Diary'. In these stories I have depicted the jealousy of a woman towards another woman of her own status and level. Do you think men are not jealous? As men are jealous towards their own colleagues, classmates and men of their own stature and position, so are women. It is not true that men are free from jealousy.

"But a male-writer makes a mistake when he depicts a woman. For example, sex is very important for a man. It is the highest kind of joy and happiness for him. But for a woman it is not so. A man can enjoy the body of a woman even if he doesn't love her. But for a woman it is entirely different. A boy forgets his duties towards his mother as soon as he marries, while a girl cannot forget her mother. As soon as a wife dies, a husband can forget her and marry another woman. But a woman cannot forget her husband even if she has been married to him for a few months only. A woman cannot detach herself easily, while a man can renounce his wife and children and become a *sādhu*!

"The male-writer cannot understand this basic difference between a man and a woman. He thinks only of what is possible or easy for a man to do or what a man likes to do. But an act or deed or behaviour which comes naturally to man can be very difficult for a woman. A man is not capable of understanding a woman fully. At least a woman writer cannot do this kind of injustice to her woman-character."

I said to her, "Your story *Brahmā-jī-Bhūlā* is very famous. It is a tragic story about a woman, who does her best to become a decent member of the society, but fails miserably as her mother was a woman of ill-fame. By becoming a prostitute, she takes a terrible revenge on the society by ruining the home-life of each and every man who comes into contact with her. This story reminds one of Zola's *Nana*. Where did you get the idea of this story from?" She said," I have not heard about Zola's novel. I have heard about it from you today for the first time. To tell you the truth. I have studied and read Sindhi, Sanskrit and Hindi literature only. I have read only a few novels in English like *Thelma, Pride and Prejudice, Prodigal Son, Le Miserable*. I read these novels when I was very young and my school teachers used to tell us to read them. But I was not able to understand them. I had to seek the help of my cousins even to understand the stories or the themes of these novels. Actually we girls were not supposed to read novels in those times. And so, it was difficult for us to lay hands on fictional writings.

"After the partition of the country, things changed and we did not have to seek our elders' permission to read the novels. Books were also easily available. I took fancy for Perry Mason's detective novels. Each day, I would finish one book and thus I devoured almost all his novels. Afterwards, though there were no restrictions on me, I preferred essays of serious type or philosophical books to novels or stories.

"I have written three stories on the theme of the fallen women: *Brahmā-jī-Bhūlā* (Brahma's Blunder), *Hane-Ta-Hooakujh-bi-Na-Huee* (Today, She is a Junk) and *Shahnaz*. In Sind I had read a small booklet written by a Muslim woman who had an affair with the son of a noble man. The boy grew up into a politician and became the Chief Minister of Sind. Needless to say, the girl was discarded by him and she became a prostitute who was visited by men from the high society only. Once the son of that Chief Minister, a college student visited her. She was shocked to see him. She was moved to write something about the destiny of the girls who fall in love with boys of the upper class.

"This book entitled *The Romance of a Hur* left a lasting impression on my mind because of the true and sincere feelings expressed in it by that lady. She wrote, we are just like dustbins. These wealthy men throw away their excess-sex in us and we have to accept their filth. Then they call us filthy. Yes, we are filthy dustbins. But, if these filthy dust-bins do not exist, the honour of the respected ladies would be in danger. Where will the men with excess-sex throw their filth? I got the idea of writing on the fallen women from this book."

Then I turned to the feminist movement and said, "You have depicted the oppression and suppression of women in society, but you have also displayed the weaknesses of the fair sex. Do you think that the problems faced by Indian women would be solved only if they followed in the foot-steps of their western counterparts or the so-called women's libbers?"

She replied emphatically, "No, Indian women won't be successful in solving their social problems if they follow the liberation movement of the western women. In the western countries the concept of a family is very different from the Indian concept of a family. In the West, family means husband and wife and children, but in India one's mother, father, sisters, brothers are very much included in the family. The Western woman's idea of marriage, sex, family, husband and bringing up of children is different from that of the Indian woman's. Actually an Indian woman is not tied down in legal rules. She is ruled by social customs and conventions because they are linked with religion. As far as an Indian woman is concerned, legal laws are not so powerful in the social sphere as the social customs are. In our country a married son is not expected to touch the feet of his mother but his wife is bound to do so. In our country mothers willingly sacrifice their own comforts to look after their children. But in the West, the mothers are not expected to sacrifice their own entertainment. They must take time off for their hair-care, make-up, concerts, balls etc. If a mother in London goes to a cocktail party leaving her small kids alone, nobody thinks that she has failed in her duty. Then, in the Western countries, a husband is always expected to help his wife with the household chores. The Western woman, if she happens to lose her husband, never thinks of remaining a widow for life. She cannot postpone her re-marriage even for the sake of her children. There, a woman gives priority to her physical appearance, even when she is old."

Popati further added, "In India men make fun of a woman if she speakes of freedom. A husband gets angry when his wife speaks of women's lib. In my opinion, men in India are afraid of the freedom of women. If women are free, men would lose their rights and privileges along with numerous comforts and conveniences they have enjoyed for centuries. But the funny side of this is that men think that when a woman becomes aware of her capabilities, she stops being a woman! Herein lies their faulty thinking. I think the word 'Freedom' is misconceived. Freedom from whom? Freedom from what? In fact woman of India has chained herself to her own misconceived ideas. There are a number of shackles around her. Today, these shackles are rusted but she is not aware of the rust. So she has to awaken from her slumber. She has to know the things in their true perspective and colours. She has to recognise her own self. That can happen only when she throws fear out of her mind."

Enquiring about her favourite writers, I said, "Who are the writers, I mean the Indian writers, you are fond of?" She replied "I am very fond of Kalidasa. I started writing only after reading his works. Then the works of such writers as Jayashankar Prasad, Maithilisharan Gupta and Mahadevi Varma captivated my heart. I like Krishna Chandar also. Of course, I am fond of Sindhi poets like Shah Abdul Latif and Sachal. I have also enjoyed reading Sheikh-Ayaz, Niyaz Humayun, Tanveer-Abasi, Sameerah Zameen, Ghulam Nabi Mughul, etc."

Then I brought up the question of the translation of literary works. I said, "Every writing is imprisoned in its own language and script. Only those who know that particular language and script can get the pleasure of reading it. Don't you think that translating great works from one language into other language is a worthwhile work?"

She said, "As far as the script is concerned, Sahitya Akademi published the works of Gurudev Tagore, in transliterated Devanagari script. But the attempt failed because if one knows the Devanagari Script only, one cannot read a book written in the Bengali language or in any other language for that matter. Until and unless one knows the language itself, one cannot read a book by merely knowing the script. Hence translation of such works is the only way. A great work in any modern language of India should be translated either into Hindi or into English and also into other modern Indian languages. But when this kind of work is undertaken by a Government body or a semi-Government institution, corruption steps in. In that case translation work is given to a person who knows only one language. And he plays havoc with the original writing. A right choice of the translator and the work alone can serve the readers and the literary world."

Winding up our discussion, I said, "You must be well aware of present state of literary criticism in our country. Do you think that this sort of criticism can be any good to the writer or the reader?"

She said, "The right to criticise must go to a scholar or a knowledgeable person. And that person must be free from partiality and prejudice. In a microscopic community of the Sindhis, the critics are writers themselves. Their self-involvement and interests have resulted in the formation of groups among the writer-critics. For example, in the fifties (1947-1955) the progressive writers read and praised only the writers of their group. They did not care to read the writings of others. Similarly the writers (writers of anti-literature) of today, do not like to go through the writings of those other than their own friends. They may not praise each other but they recognise only their friends as writers worth naming in their literary criticism."

(Bombay—5.1.1984)

Krishna Sobti

B. 18.2.1925, Gujarat (now in Pakistan); *mt.* Punjabi *edn.* in Delhi, Shimla and Lahore; *car.* teaching, Govt. service, now writing; *Awards & hons.* Sahitya-Shiromani Award, 1980, Fellow, Punjabi Uni., 1980-82, Sahitya Akademi Award*, 1980, Hindi Akademi Delhi Award, 1982, Fellow, Sahitya Akademi, since 1996, Maithili-sharan Gupta National Sammān, 1996-97; *pubs. Hindi short story collections* Yāron Ke Yār, Tin Pahār, 1968, Bādalon ke Ghere, 1980, Ai Ladki, 1991, *novels* Dār Se Bichhudī, 1958, Mitro Marjānī, 1966, Surajmukhī Andhere Ke, 1972, *Zindagināmā—Zindā Rukh, 1979, Dilo-Dānish, 1993, *misc.* Ham Hashmat, 1977, Sobti: Ek Sohbat (Rep. writings), 1989, *English* (in trans.) Mitro Marjani, Blossoms in the Dark; *Russian* (in trans.) Mitro Marjani; many successful stage presentations of this novel and filming of the story 'Sikka Badal Gaya'; her writings have been translated in many Indian languages also.

Author's Integrity is Supreme

"Friends, every writer is a writer for himself, by himself. If he struggles endlessly, fights against adversities head on, he obliges none else except his own pen. Any genuine writer would write for values, not for those who only clamour for values. Had it not been so, writers and artists would have ended up as decorative pieces displayed in canopies and Vigyan Bhavans". These bitter realisations come from none other than the frank and fearless fiction writer Krishna Sobti whose writings rise on our literary and social horizon as prominent happenings. Her earlier fictions *Dar se Bichhudi* (Separated from the Flock) and *Badalon ke Ghere* (Envelopments of Clouds) became the big events of Hindi literature as also the recent ones *Ai Ladki* (O, Girl) and *Dilo-Danish* (Heart and intellect that tend to shake up the society to its roots.)

The creative excitement, the critical turmoil and the socio-ethical debates stirred up by her novels *Mitro Marjani, Yaron ke Yar* and *Suraj Mukhi Andhere ke* during the last four decades have not faded out yet. The urge for getting to the roots of the socio-ethical do's and dont's, inhibitions and limitations imposed by the society as reflected in Krishna Sobti's works baffles both modern feminists and blind traditionalists. When Mitro, the heroine of her novel *Mitro Marjani* came out with the vocal expression of her physical and biological needs not only the traditionalists got wild with rage, the theorists of feminism were also astounded.

Krishna Sobti believes, "The authenticity of any literary piece is related not only to the author's basic approach to life, but also to the strength of her creative flight revealed in the physique, nature and sturdy bones of her characters. Couching her characters in their natural and plausible language, she lends them such dimensions in their own idiom as could not have been possible without deep emotional sensitivity. Her linguistic capabilities know no parallel in lending motion, pulsation and flight to reality by transcending the mystic boundaries of the surreal."

Her creations seem to bridge the gap between the audio and visual literature. Her novel *Mitro Marjani* has gone into sixty-seven stage presentations. The staging of *Dār se Bichhudi* and filming of *Sikkā Badal Gayā*, besides posing a challenge, became a source of creative inspiration to many stage personalities.

Many awards and honours have come Sobti's way, but they could not disturb her stride. She got Sahitya Akadami Award in 1980 on her magnum opus 'Zindaginama'. Besides, she has received Shiromani award and Sahitya Kala Parishad award, the latest being the Maithlisharan Gupta Sahitya Award for 1996-97.

Interviewing her on literature, particularly her own writings, is an experience in itself. Though it took us long to manage an exclusive sitting, we were totally lost in conversation for hours when we met. My opening query was, "Your writings commenced with poetry, but it was fiction which brought you fame and perhaps creative satisfaction also. Did you find poetry inadequate to express yourself satisfactorily that you switched over to fiction as a medium?"

She was frank as usual and replied, "The intense sensual world that a born poet has to visualise and maintain within himself or herself ran counter to my nature and seemed beyond me. The only saving grace was that I had the instinct to realise my limitations. The inherent intensity in poetry so essential for a poetic flight was difficult to acquire because of my cold and forthright nature. The sense of individualness that had taken deep roots in me made it almost difficult to endure the dual personalities. Thus, the brief spell of this state passed away almost unnoticed, something left over was only some good lines of poetry which hovered around me at times. A line of poetry that enlivens your whole being need not necessarily be your own. That which reveals you to yourself or connects you to your being could be anybody's and could touch your inmost sensitivity."

"The imagery of any sensitive poet was difficult to suit a prose writer like me to whom the very earth she tramples on was her sky also. A line of a poem, a bunch of words, a piece of emotional experience and their intense possibility ended much earlier. It is, no doubt, painful to the prose writer, though not so much. It has to be accepted that the emergence of a poet or a poem cannot be brought about with efforts alone. The clarity of prose, its social and mental forthrightness has always drawn me and has also opened up the innermost self for my writer."

"Understating the implications of the language and creative truth of the meaning of words, their beat, charm, generosity, excitement—they all inspire mental intensity and glow an invaluable asset for human expression. The element of genious a writer is gifted with is always in proportion to his capacity and to this is related the writer's sensibility, intellectual background and fathomless impersonalness."

"Thinking and writing in unidimensional language bores me. As a writer I have to transcend myself, despite being at the creative centre of the language. Moulding the language and its idioms according to his characters, pushing himself to the background tentamounts not only to experimentation but it also reveals the capability of the writer. This capability expands the creative sensibilities both for the writer and the reader. Writer's self-analysis and self-realisation, passing through this process, develops into artistic skill".

Coming to the development of characterization in her works, I asked, "During the creation of your characters you must have felt many a time that you are nearing the truth. Would you like to provide us a glimpse into your creative mind from this point of view when Mitro or Ratti were taking shape within you".

She thought for a while and dug deep into her inmost recesses, "During my complex creative process I keep on listening to and picking the slightest signals travelling from inner to outer as well as outer to inner realms of my being. To identify inner conflicts and self-contradictions you have to measure the basic geography and history of the situations. You cannot lend them life by a mere touch of whimsical imagination. To recreate a point of time imagination alone is not enough, nor would ideological tinge suffice. If I may say about myself, I have not been able to produce anything merely from imagination removed from realities.

"The writer's attitude to life is essential for any important creative work. It is also significant to know whether you are accustomed to see and examine things with your own eyes or you try to identify them by distancing yourself from them. Whether you are accustomed to see and search outside on the basis of the stamp of relationship put on you. In your capacity as a writer do you measure the wholeness of life and literature by situations alone? Do you start projecting your own inquiries considering them to be those emerging from the depths of the human mind? The writer must transcend these limitations. Communicability of the content cannot be the only justification. The human mind can spring a surprise or be surprised at any turn, any moment.

"Many fluctuations come across in highly complex situations and happenings. At the bottom of these lies much that does not meet the eye. You have to delve deeper and deeper like a diver to get at what is called 'truth'. The revelation of truth does not lie in cleverness. The discreet writer creates within him a sanctum-sanctorium, besides his personal knowledge and experience, and presents the artistic whole relevant to the specific writing. My truth is the whole truth, this obduracy removes the author far away from the fountain-head called absolute truth.

"If analysed, truth is reflected not only in the personality of our character, it is also hidden under the masks they put on as a matter of right. The distance from and closeness to them is that point from which the author can gauge his run. If the writer is in control of himself, the character progresses ahead with its incomplete existence. If you control your distance from or closeness to the character, you help the writer within you. The creativity of a writing does not lie in description alone. Alertness, mental awareness, inner vision are the basic demand of a writing. The quality of a writer's mental faculties transform even the false evidence into the so-called truth".

Expecting her to elaborate her creative process in the context of her famous character Mitro, I asked, "Tell us something about the emergence of Mitro. She must have taken long to take shape within you?"

She opened up gradually, "You have inquired about Mitro. The restlessness of the individual that Mitro symbolises is not only the exuberant sex, it also reflects the identity of the woman often forgotten in the glorification by the family. Her eulogy is confined only to her role as a manual labourer and provider of physical satisfaction. Before writing Mitro I had no idea of the negative of her photograph or what print it would produce. It was just once that I had a glimpse of a lively body like a bed of greenery, standing near a domestic animal and carrying a heavy load on her head, with a look of longing and a bulge under her breast, covering her wheatish blossoming body draped in long skirt and shawl (Lehanga and Odhani), a unique figure of flesh and blood enveloped in silvery shine, a primitive look in the wistful eyes, putting on airs and wearing a stud in her tiny nose. Her neck turned slightly straight towards the bushes. Noticing the contractor passing by, she hurled a small pebble, 'Don't dare throw a glance this side, Oh Thekadara. If stuck up in my skirt, you would be lost for good.' Shyness ran all over the face of the middle-aged contractor. He retorted recovering from his embarrassment, 'You are deluding yourself, you low cast. If I pierce through your elusive effeminacy supreme, all your virtuosity will fall flat and you will run amuck.' throwing a hint by tilting her skirt, she lashed out like a bolt from the blue, 'You must worship this Sharbati. Then only you would be free from your insatiable lust.'

"The writer was silent with his white collared ego. There is no ban on prattling. Whatever is spoken, it floats in the air, or stops suddenly, may be caught or gets lost at the back of the mind. Pushing aside the suspense of the writer a chain of questions kept on whispering into his ears—which one is greater, body or mind? You talk of the mind, but greet the body; the entire universe stands on this burning tip. The body that emits fragrance, it is through this that the inherent treasure of soul is cultivated. It is the body always that becomes the medium of all sublimation. If the soul is enshrined in the body, is it not just a sheer vanity to ignore it? Awakening and exciting this old plateau with her touch Misri Bai's Chunnari kept on swinging the feast of colours.

"One fine evening, God knows under what wisdom, the writer identified that current beyond the smoky look of the contractor and with a view to freezing the shot, had the folly of taking the initiative of digging deep into the background of that encounter. In hesitation leaf after leaf went on flying in the air and the time between the unborn writing and the writer stretched out. Again in one cold night of winter, passing through an old dilapidated colony, my steps came to a grinding halt. A sound of crying, shrieking filled my ears, 'Mom, take your son to a physician. He is not capable of performing the frolicsome act.' Then sounds of thrashing followed by the same cry, 'Kill me and bury me under the earth. I will get rid of at least this anguish.'

"Stunned, the writer began thinking—why is it that, the same old issue is being reopened? I heard this dialogue earlier also somewhere—some mild complaint, some blemish—no cover up, only that what has been expressed. Whose fault is it after all? A desire without the body. The thirst which it reflects, why hate that longing from yourself to the other, from the other to yourself, two sides of the same primitive rhythm. In the thrill of the twin moment, faces of the two identities merged into one. Are they capable of standing this double collision—denial and acceptance at two different levels? What would be the capacity of this demand? How strong would be this throbbing desire which is beyond the scope of sin and virtuosity and much above their protectors.

"Pushing aside any romantic imagination the writer's eyes stuck to the door-sill of a single family. First of all what met my eyes was the ventilator of the house, then an old umbrella, followed by Gurudas lying on the bed and Dhanvanti sitting by the hearth and then shadows of the daughters-in-law, peeping out from inside. One can see only that much as the insight is capable of. One can touch only as much as one digs deep. From behind the shutters of the household Mitro provided a glance, studying the surroundings in her alertness, laughing and playing jokingly, opening and exposing the antiquity of her being a woman, awakening it with her discretion ... the court-yard of the house-hold becomes the stage, a complete world in itself. But how can a world be complete merely by its existence? They are bound by the fire and fragrance of give and take which throbs in the form of figures of flesh and blood."

I inched gradually towards the inherent primitive urge clothed in Mitro and observed, "Mitro Marjani has assumed the proportions of a classic novel. She attracts us despite her impertinence. She is that woman of flesh and blood which is highly complex in her transparency, also very harsh in her very humaneness. She doesn't spare anybody, doesn't excuse anyone. She shows every one his place. Facing the challenges posed by others, she has herself become a challenge for all. It is perhaps for this that she is denied justice, both by her mother and her creator, the writer. First of all you infused into her unbound physical desire and then sealed all the outlets of her fulfilment in the garb of social propriety, forcing her to suffocate in the four walls of the house-hold. What will happen after all to the unending thirst of Mitro, the unique creation of yours?"

Sobti went into introspection again, "The fragrance of Mitro can be had from anywhere in the courtyard of any house-hold. But it was only the middle daughter-in-law of Gurudas's family who could earn the affectionate title of 'Mitro Marjani', not through author's favour but in her own right. Mitro stares at life on her own strength, offers jestful comments, quarrels, collides, frightens and also indulges in high-handedness.... During one challenging moment seeing her mother's prestige going to dogs, she distinguishes the body from clothes and gathering her fluttering clothes returns to herself from the other extreme, identifies herself.

"The author had nothing preplanned while writing it out. The story revealed itself automatically and laid bare layer after layer. The waves and strides of the body and mind, love and entreaties, quarrels and frictions all got entwined in the rhythm and musical pattern of the household. The blazing primitive fire in Mitro, verbal bouts with her younger and elder sisters-in-law. Holding the family altogether by Gurudas and Dhanvanti even at this old age, lost in the struggling time spent together forced to stitch together the seams of the family—family, a world in itself. But no family is complete in itself just by its existence. The inherent earthquakes keep on rocking its structure, foundations and beams. When an earthquake erupts in the form of a Mitro, it is bound to develop into the fiction *Mitro Marjani.* It is not the outcome of just the writers' skill and interaction of various incidents. It is the culmination of the friction and collision of different social values, very much within the framework of the house-hold.

"At the creative level, no authenticity springs only from the factual information, craft or the capability of its flight. It is very much related to physical structure, behaviour pattern and basic nature of its characters. In the absence of these qualities a writing may distinguish itself for its craft, polish and make up, but no life would throb in its micro and macro organism. Mitro is not just a creation of imagination. That is why the more the bends and turns in the life and soul of Mitro, the more the strength in her for headon collisions, the more the imposition of restrictions on the author. The author played his or her role not in controlling the flooded stream called Mitro, overflowing and demolishing its banks, but to facilitate her a free flow.

"Any emphasis on ideals or sins was enough to label Mitro as asocial. The sexual contexts wriggling before her and the far-reaching sense of security could not be interchanged at any cost, this was enough for the author to understand. With her inborn playfulness, fascinating outspokenness, physical energy coupled with smartness and ready wit, Mitro stepped towards the threshold of the house without sounding the author. But the author found it neither alarming nor surprising or irrelevant. On one side the thirst of Mitro's healthy and stout body is unnatural, while on the other side her awareness of the family ties has sharpened. Mitro has proved through her decisiveness that at the level of thinking also she posseses abundant commonsense which endears her to the readers, despite her discourteous and naughty behaviour. The very social border from which her playful subtlety has sprouted, has infused in her both the sour and sweet nature missing in the other daughters-in-law of Gurudas's family.

"It would be worthwhile to remember that just to narrate is not fiction. On the contrary, the fiction creates and reveals the abstract. Creation of the visual world takes place in the inner space of the mind. The writer is settled so deep that he just disappears from the surface. We have to differentiate between the inner turbulence of the writer and the outer social clamour."

Taking up her another important novel *Suraj-mukhi Andhere ke* (Sun-flowers of Darkness), I remarked, "I wonder whether the heroine Ratti of this novel is an extension of Mitro, despite the fact that she had to suffer from a sense of guilt right from the childhood. Maybe Ratti had not to confront the social ethics, but she did have a deep-rooted inhibition to be overcome, besides the immense thirst for sex and a strong desire to become mother."

Reacting sharply, she observed, "Ratti and Mitro are not the outcome of psychological complexes of the author. The characters grapple with the situations that confront them. In the very middle of their sojourns stand the aggressive accidents which never fail to extract from them the price of their very existence. Essentially, the writer is not what his or her characters are and even the characters are not what the writer is, though the vision that identifies them is that of the writer. It is here that the inner vision of the writer assumes significance. It is important to remember that during his creative venture the writer is neither on his being nor on verification exclusively. His creation should be considered neither merely his intellectual intervention, nor the infusion of his own ethical values".

I probed further, "Ratti's restless concern for getting rid of her wounded past reflects her vigour. She is not the type of girl who would even concede her failure and give up. Her suffocating loneliness is as real as her desire to get rid of it. But Divakar's offer to serve as a medium of her fulfilment does not strike a chord of plausibility. It lends affectation. In her attempt to emancipate from the sense of guilt, his role is not that of a participant, but as a medium reducing the major event to a one-sided affair. I wonder how Ratti, a self-respecting girl that she is, could accept this role of Divakar, prompted perhaps by compassion."

Sobti dug deep into my interpretation and replied, "Surrounded by the physical haziness, she remained detached. Her physical and mental ailments would have been sufficient to drag her personality into the dense cloudiness, but Ratti never lost her inner void and outer search, rather kept her alert which is a great quality in itself. It is also not insignificant that she kept her intrinsic desire intact even by outer means. She did not sacrifice her delicate and subtle primitive desire at the alter of segmented social blockade. She did not even allow herself to be dominated wholly by the instinct of individualisation.

"Ratti's struggle is against the wave that lashes at her body rippling fast from mind to body and body to mind of the person and becomes the grammer of his sensibility. Ratti could have turned a rebel, breaking all the disciplines. But she kept up her struggle for freedom from loneliness and boredom. The incident like rape and its ugly consequences which gripped her with cold and rocky desolation of virginity, were sufficient to pin down any child, a boy or girl, to a terror-stricken future. Any psychological ailment could have injected into the body and mind arithmetic of subtle segmentation. But Ratti was brave enough not to cut her from herself even in this highly charged state of shattering alienation.

"The moment of being with Divakar and merging herself with his being in the rare state of dissolution, which she had earned, could not have allowed him to be a mere medium, as Ratti had herself been a part of his thrillless boring married life. This led to the flow of the bliss between them. The fact that no such desire as to extract something more awakened in Ratti, signifies spontaneity in the pure and peaceful 'self' of Ratti. It was at the level of the body that a pious feeling could have been awakened and realised, forgetting the unfortunate incident of rape. To the culmination of this act it is not the inner longing of Ratti and the manliness of Divakar that would have contributed, but the art of consummation coupled with the fellow feeling would have also facilitated that perhaps, that much was the run of the story."

Coming to her epic work *Zindaginama, Zinda Rukh* which has the tinge of a regional novel, I observed, "This novel which has assumed epic proportions, is just superb. You told me once that its writing, re-writing and publishing has a long history. Would you tell us about it?"

It was painful for her to recall its history, "This novel was written in 1953 under the little 'Channa'. The manuscript was presented to Bharati Bhandar, Allahabad. Soon came the reply, "Your manuscript has been reviewed. It turns out to be a good novel. Congratulations, Bharati Bhandar will publish it soon." It took very long, about 25 years, for this letter of Vachaspati Misra to materialise.

"It so happened that Bharati Bhandar started printing the novel without showing its proofs to the author i.e. me. Dozens of words were changed, as they claimed improved upon, e.g. 'Shahni' was changed to 'Shahpatni', 'Kaka' to 'Lallu' 'Rukh' to 'Vriksha' 'Chhanh' to 'Chaya' and so on. All the 'improvements' were of this nature. When the printed form came, the author's anxiety set in. Bharati Bhandar was considered to be the best publishing concern those days. There was nothing new for them to accord literary touch to the manuscript of a novice writer. Being the writer of her first novel, the author entered into her own verification and found that it was difficult for her to accept the changed form of the original words. The author settled the matter at her own cost. The printed forms were destroyed. The author had to suffer the loss for the whims of the proof-reader.

"The manuscript was withdrawn. It was locked in a box. It was re-written after many years and got published in 1979 under the title 'Zindaginama'.

"The first manuscript written under the title 'Channa' was kindly seen by a 'Agneyaji'. Upendranath Ashka and Kamaleshwar were kind enough to go through its press copy. All the arrangements for publishing through Navin Press were made by B.P. Thakur of Bharati Bhandar. Yet this novel could not be reprinted.

"This manuscript was reopened at the behest of Smt. Sheela Sandhu of Rajkamal Prakashan. But a few hours thereafter it disappeared from the author's desk and got re-locked in the box. The author decided that it would have to be re-cast without looking at the old manuscript.

"It would be interesting in this context to quote the relevant excerpts from Vachaspati Pathak's letter of 1978: "Sobtiji, 'Hashmat' reminded me of the book which I was going to ruin inadvertently through my sheer stupidity. I wish you to release the book. I would be happy if it gets published. This lapse on my part keeps on haunting me. I earnestly desire that you offer this book to Loke Bharati for publishing so that they bring it out soon, and I am atoned."

Giving a turn to the discussion, I asked, "Had you been 'Krishna' instead of 'Krishnā', do you think your heroines Mitro, Ratti and Mahak would have taken the same shape as the present one?"

Welcoming the question, she remarked, "If 'Krishna' and 'Krishnā' are not the same, then Sobti has in her both. It can be said with confidence that elongation or shortening of one's name cannot change one's way or spirit of living.

"The language of feeling, experiencing and understanding as well as probing which enlightens life with a particular *Sanskar* is not only the exclusive attribute of the masculine or feminine gender of grammar, but also the result of that orderliness of effective discipline of human sensibility which develops from the source point of their own mental environment, irrespective of their sex.

"To live the surrounding creativity of life, and also to investigate it in writer's own style requires a rigorous discipline, simplicity of experience, cold and hot detachment which comes neither to any Krishna, nor Krishnā automatically. What a person is, what he lives, what he gropes for and collects, what he threads to create from the inner to the outer self, is not determined by the name and sex.

"This issue can be discussed to any extent, pleaded for and against, but nothing would be achieved or produced at the level of writing. Human dialogue and sensitivities transcend and transgress physical limitations and also the strength and weakness of ones nature. If sharpness is analysed on the basis of sex, the creative perspective will not always be right. It is well known that the works of average male writer do not essentially measure up to the strict yard stick of good literature—they are found equally emotional, shallow and superficial. Basically, the classifications are right or wrong to the extent they are affected by the thinking, the *Sanskar* and the surrounding social and intellectual climate."

Then, I took up her unique work *Ai, Ladki* (O Girl) which has been discussed immensely. I observed, "This work of yours opens up at various levels, at two in particular. In this intense dialogue between the mother and the daughter, the daughter assumed, I think, the role of a psychoanalyst and provokes the mother again and again, attempting to bring her to a mental state, called 'free association' in psychoanalysis. This results in the mother's stream of consciousness in which she starts reliving not only her own past, but also of the woman as a whole in her various roles as mother, wife, daughter, daughter-in-law etc., underlining the essential roles of woman in building up family and society and also bridging the generation gap. Do you find any substance in this contention?"

My question prompted her to relive the last phase of her mother before she passed away. Slowly she opened up, "You have yourself remarked that the story unfolds mainly at two levels. The two levels created by the disease and the doctor, one who has to leave and the others who stay on. The time when this division takes place is highly acute and painful. Then, their eyes emit a signal that we are on this side and you are on the other. It appeared then for the first time that there is something that moves her away from us and is withdrawing herself. She was a woman full of grit and endurance. She was looking in her own way at that great moment which for others was nearly over. But she communicated with the doctors and nurses attending to her with a sense of awareness. Next to them were her children, her kith and kin. Then I was for the first time convinced of her teaching, which was the outcome of her own life style, that you are on your own, you are your own in your individuality. Anyone may influence you, but if you want to be on your own you must stand up to achieve that. This was the spirit she inculcated in her children. I realised suddenly that I possess the language that can express those great moments she lived. I saw how she was bringing her near meaningfulness, approaching her end. It occurred to me that I should also visualise how she faced that moment. I remembered her symbolic saying 'the lamp will go on burning, the lamp will go on burning, the lamp will go on burning,' along with her assertion: 'I built up my family with great pains, made them to adhere to punctuality, left no stone unturned for anyone. But I never built anything for myself.' In those words I spotted the woman who was and is even now far ahead of our times. I sensed, now that we are at two different ends, this woman says that what she could not, even as she desired, do during her life time, has to be done by me and for me right now in my own life. I realised for the first time that there was much behind the image of this household lady and I must probe into it. It was the awareness of that woman, though older than me, that was ahead of me in many ways."

I probed further, "In this stream of consciousness of the mother which flows at various levels there appears to be a self contradiction. At one level she makes it known to the daughter that if latter could develop her independent personality, the credit for that goes to her parents who never discriminated between sons and daughters and treated them equally. But at the other level, in her last moments she awaits impatiently for the arrival of her son and at every small or big sound opens her eyes and asks whether he had come, as if the presence of her daughter was not enough and she wanted to leave her body in the safe hands of her son only. Haven't you noticed this contradiction?"

Sobti replied, "There is nothing odd in the episode you have pointed out, as this is not a minor *sanskar*. It is such a deep-rooted *sanskar* that cannot be questioned. In this context, I would like to relate an interesting incident. Three-four days after she passed away and when her final rites were being performed, a young woman vehemently argued with her mother within our hearing that the time had come when the daughters should also have the right, like their brothers, to perform the final rites of their parents. On hearing her I wondered why this idea came to her. She had in fact raised this issue in another context.

"I must add at this juncture that there is essentially a nearness between the father and the son. The entire culture binds them together. Being the head of the family, the father knows the culture and uses it in the interest of the family. Later, that very son becomes his staunch rival when he attains adulthood and gets married. Then the father delegates gradually his rights to the son. You would have noticed that struggle for power occurs between the father and the son only. On the other hand, the warmth of relationship between the mother and the daughter continue as the latter has to leave for another house and her development is steered, keeping this fact in view. The girl herself develops her desires and ambitions in this framework. This is an interesting but at the same time deep-rooted *sanskar*. Not only in India, to some extent in other countries also this situation prevails. But now it is possible there to transcend this, whereas it is difficult here in our country to overcome it. This is one of the major reasons for the breaking down of our joint family system."

Just another point came to my mind and I asked, "Would it be appropriate to call this work a story, as it has been projected, particularly when it contains an intense dialogue almost exclusively?"

Sobti quipped, "There is no insistence from my side to call *Ai Ladki* a story, Despite its being conversational, there is something in this episode which accords it the form of a long story. It would not be wrong to say that had it been written in the form of a play, it would have been better. Dialogue was the demand of this simple but extraordinary situation.

"It was a matter of concern for me that the writers' limitation did not allow it to take the form of a play. It is the ambition of a prose-writer to write at least one play during his creative period. I must accept my inability that his could not happen.

"The practice of day to-day living cannot be termed as continuity. The presence of a terminal disease contains in itself a dramatic situation which is the final chapter of the human body and mind. And such dramatic situations are not part of a day to-day living. When I thought of capturing this episode, it occurred to me that such a dramatic situation be presented in the form of a play. But later I realised that I did not possess the skill to mould it into a play and thus, I was constrained to write it as a story, admitting as to why should I spoil my work because of my limitations."

Coming to the concluding question, I observed, "Your latest novel *Dilo-Danish* deals with a lively yet subtle relationship between the master Kripanarayan and his keep Mahak and that too in a balanced manner. This balance could be maintained, I think, because Kripanarayan happened to be the head of a traditional and large joint family and it had become his second nature to look after all the members of his family even at his own cost, though he never considered Mahak and her son and daughter as a part of his family. We come across a full-fledged joint family in both 'Mitro Marjani' and 'Zindaginama'. This prompts me to ask you what is your concept of a joint family, its importance and significance?

She was apprehensive of Kripanarayan's role as the head of this large family, "He cannot be viewed at all as a simple and ideal head of the family. The proportions in which a head of the family and a lawyer are blended in his personality transform him into a phychological case, if not a complex psychological puzzle. Under the cover of propriety he exploits his wife and other family members to suit his own interest. In the name of the same propriety he ignores Mahak to strengthen his own rights. With his inherent male strategy and skill sometimes he creates controversies and sometimes settles them himself. Sometimes with great wisdom and skill he cleverly surrenders himself under the cover of ethical values just to reduce his own tension. In spite of all that, whatever qualities and weaknesses this 'Vakil Sahib' possess, these have been inset in his personality in such a composite manner that his positive and negative traits cannot be identified separately and distinctly.

"In the form of the Vakil Sahib he springs up an intensive personality. The delusion of his strong points and weaknesses, his reasonings and illogicality run hand-in-hand safely and timely. He also possesses a lawyer's investigative skill and foresight as also the acumen of resolving problematic situations. His position as the head of the family allows him to hold his personal court. He is his own lawyer and pleads for and against his mind and intellect in his best interest. He himself stands for his valued witness. He himself frames the charges and also provides the evidence himself. He also projects the fake idea that he can catch the thief hidden in anybody's mind. He enforces do's and don'ts in the household systematically and does not hesitate to use his prerogative. In his personality pure passion and its appearance coexist without transgressing the situation. The fence protecting the joint family always dominates and usurps others rights politely. It may be termed as the duty of the head of the family or the duty to oneself.

"He did almost nothing for Mahak. Consequently, the family outside his household remained secondary. Through this relationship Badru, the son of Vakil Sahib and Mahak, got added to the basic capital of the family. The reason for keeping Mahak's jewellery box out of the family treasure also prevailed in turning it out again. But the step taken by Mahak which took the form of her stubbornness put a question mark on the birth-right and authority of Kripanarayan, the Vakil Sahib.

"Exploitation of one individual by another is found not only outside the family but also in the family itself. In fact, it starts from the family itself. Family is a spinal cord in which the whole human family appears to be throbbing and squirming as one world, but is not one in reality. Negative noise, nobility, sobriety, courtesy and reprimand, insult, forbidance are enough to cripple a weak person. The stress and strains of the complexities of a joint family are the factors responsible for its disintegration."

(New Delhi—19.4.1994)

*

Kapila Vatsyayan

B. 25.12.1928, Delhi; *mt.* Panjabi; *edn.* M.A. from University of Delhi in English Literature and from University of Michigan in Education and English, Ph.D. in Indology from Banaras Hindu University, Varanasi; *Car.* presently Academic Director, Indira Gandhi National Centre for the Arts, New Delhi, and President of India International Centre, New Delhi; Member-Secretary, Indira Gandhi National Centre for the Arts, New Delhi 1990-93; Secretary, Department of Arts, Ministry of Human Resource Development, Government of India, New Delhi 1985-90; Additional Secretary, Department of Culture 1982-85; Short Term Visiting Professor, University of Philadelphia 1981; Short Term Visiting Professor, University of Columbia 1979-80; Joint

Educational Adviser, Ministry of Education 1975-82; Deputy Educational Adviser, Department of Culture 1964-74; Joint Secretary, XXVI International Congress of Orientalists 1962-64; Assistant Educational Adviser, Ministry of Education 1954-62; Faculty of English, University of Delhi 1949-54. *Awards & Honours*: Fellow of Sangeet Natak Akademi New Delhi, 1970; Jawaharlal Nehru Memorial Fellowship 1975; Manipuri Akademi of Dance, Drama and the Arts, 1978; Campbell Award of the Asiatic Society of Bombay 1980; R.P. Chanda Centenary Medal of the Asiatic Society Calcutta 1982; Manipuri Sangeet Sahitya Akademi, 1985; Padma Shri of Republic of India, 1990; Srimanta Sankardeva Award from State Government of Assam, 1990; Life Fellow of the Asiatic Society of Bombay, 1991; Parishad Samman from Sahitya Kala Parishad, Delhi, 1992; John D. Rockfeller III Award from Asian Cultural Council, New York, 1993; Bharat Vasundhara Samman, National Press of India Award 1994; Foreign Member, Russian Academy of Sciences, Moscow, 1994; Life Fellow, Lalit Kala Akademi, New Delhi, 1995; Honorary D.Litt. from B.H.U. Varanasi, Rabindra Bharati Calcutta, Manipuri University, Mount Holyoke College USA, Rashtriya Sanskrit Vidyapeetham, Tirupati, *Publications*: Classical Indian Dance in Literature and the Arts, 1968, 2nd edition 1977; Some Aspects of Cultural Policies in India, 1971; Indian Classical Dance, 1974, 2nd edition 1992; Traditions of Indian Folk Dance, 1976, 2nd edition in 1987; Ramayana and the Arts of Asia, 1975; Contribution in Traditional Performing Arts through the Mass Media in India, 1975; Traditional Indian Theatre: Multiple Streams, 1980 (translated into Bengali, Gujarati and Hindi in 1996); Miniatures of Gita Govinda—17th Century Manuscript of North Gujarat, 1980; The Jaur Gita Govinda, 1980; The Bundi Gita Govinda, 1981; Dance in Indian Painting, 1982; Dance Sculpture in Sarangpani Temple, 1982; The Square and the Circle of the Indian Arts, 1983; Gita Govinda in the Assam School of Painting, 1986; Mewari Gita Govinda, 1987; The Arts of Kerala Kshetram, 1989; Bharata and the *Nāṭyaśāstra*, 1996.

The Holistic Vision of the Art

To all the serious scholars of art, culture and cosmology Kapila Vatsyayan is known as one of the foremost authorities on Indology. A study of her basic works reveals her deep insights into the integral vision of art, laying emphasis on the inter-dependence and interrelationship of different manifestations of art, while accepting the separate entity of each. She puts it clearly without mincing words, "Each aspect of the art has its own integrity, yet it functions within a dimension of interdependence and interrelatedness with nature, culture, life-style, social structure and the cosmocentric world view. It is in the simultaneous perception of these interlocking categories that the holistic vision of the art becomes manifest". In this perception all disciplines, from the arts to sciences, move into a dynamic and creative oneness, posing a serious challenge to the fragmented approach to the understanding of the art, proposing at the same time an effective and yet holistic view to obviate the unending conflicts plaguing the modern society.

She was born and brought up in a family of social reformers, scholars and artists with roots in Kashmir and Panjab, her mother Satyawati Malik being *inter alia* a renowned Hindi writer. Kapilaji had her early education in Delhi, but the family soon moved to Calcutta. The home of her parents, both at Delhi and Calcutta, was a meeting place for freedom-fighters, poets, scholars, artists and musicians. A childhood spent in the atmosphere vibrating with multicreativities, with frequent visits to Shantiniketan, laid the foundation of her not only communicating with different regions, but also infused in her an incessant desire for learning the Indian arts, particularly music and dance, then considered a taboo for the middle class, especially their female children.

Though English literature and Western art were the disciplines of her formal education in Delhi University and University of Michigan, USA, she realised her deep-rooted urge for Indology during her studies abroad. It was A.K. Coomaraswamy who turned her back to India for vigorous pursuit of the Indian arts. Soon she got herself involved whole-heartedly in her research work for the Ph.D. degree in Indology from B.H.U. The *sanskāras* of her childhood, coupled with her training in the oral traditions of India, made her a communicator between the North and the South, the East and the West, the theory and the practice, the classical and the folk, the literate and the oral tradition.

Her interest in the field of dance and the art of communication through dance evolved one methodology of establishing national integration. The other was through art exhibitions in India and abroad. She played a seminal role in organising thematic exhibitions, focussing on different themes basic to the understanding of the Indian arts, as also to bring home the message of the unity and diversity.

As an Adviser in the Ministry of Education she had been associated with formulation of policy framework since the early fifties. Her senior colleagues included K.G. Saiyadain, Humayun Kabir, Prem Kirpal to mention a few. Over this long period extending to four decades she displayed a remarkable quality of being an institution builder. In these capacities she has been responsible for the establishment of many institutions such as Central Institute of Higher Tibetan Studies in Sarnath, Nehru Memorial Museum and Library, New Delhi, Centre for Cultural Relations and Training, New Delhi and School of Buddhist Studies, Leh, etc. and many others.

Her multi-disciplinary pursuits and polyvalent skill culminated in her being the author of the conceptual plan of the Indira Gandhi National Centre for the Arts, an institute that encompasses all the arts in their different aspects of interdependence and inter-webbing, the most demonstratable presentation of which was the visualisation of the unique exhibitions on *Kham* (inner and outer space), *ākāra* (form), *Kāla* (time), *prakrti* (primal elements), and *Ṛta Ṛtu* (Chaos and Order).

In her life and work, vision and performance, Kapila Vatsyayan emerges as one of the foremost authorities on the integral comprehension and methodical study of the Indian arts. She carries forward the tradition of A.K. Coomaraswamy, Vasudeva Saran Agarwal and Stella Kramrisch.

Discussing with her the basic tenets of Indology and the holistic vision of arts that she propounds is an experience in itself, though she took long to find time for the purpose out of her multifarious engagements. I set the ball rolling with my opening question, "You got your post-graduate degree in English literature and also taught English literature in the University of Delhi. What was it that inspired you to switch over to the intensive study of Indology?"

She replied, "Your query regarding my interest in Indian archaeology and antiquity is appropriate particularly so because my early education and further studies were in English Literature and Western Arts, undertaken first in India, later in USA. This change in focus of interest is to be seen not merely in the framework of Kapila—the person, but within the broad context of the historical period in which I was born and brought up. I belong to the pre-Independence generation in which English was much emphasized and accorded priority. Concurrent and complimentary was, however, my own upbringing. Whether in the Catholic Convent, Indraprastha College, Hindu College of the Delhi University or at USA studying English Literature and Western Arts, I was simultaneously exposed to the Sanskrit language and literature and also trained in music and dance and painting. The environment at home was suffused with literature. Literary people would visit the family frequently at Kashmir, Calcutta, Delhi. We travelled to seas and mountains. The annual journey from Bengal to Kashmir was the greatest education. We spoke several languages and met people of different regions, faiths and intellectual disciplines. Thus evidently, despite my association with English literature at the intellectual level I was never cut off from the India—its literature, culture and the arts, In fact, the two streams have been flowing concurrently in my life since childhood.

"After I reached USA, I continued to pursue English and American Literature, art education and modern dance. This was the hay day of the Behaviourist School. Collingwood, I.A. Richards, Cleanth Brooks were most important. I had opportunity to take courses with them. In those days, there was another intellectual in America to whom I was not personally known but whose writings influenced me tremendously. He was A.K. Coomaraswamy. Before travelling abroad, I had known Dr. Vasudev Sharan Aggarwal who later became my teacher in a more formal way. Prior to the journey to the USA there was an opportunity of great significance. At that time, an exhibition on Indian Art, known as the first Burlington Show, was being organised for England. My mother, Smt. Satyawati Malik took me to him. That time his office was above the National Archives. He exposed me to the great treasures, spoke of the heritage. As I was leaving, he gave me two pictures. One of them was of the woman writing a letter from Bhuvaneswar, the other the famous Surasundari from Khajuraho. A third was a plastar cast of the Sarnath Buddha. He said "Kapila, you are going. You may study whatever you want there but keep these in your room. Whenever you get time, look at them but not consciously. One day they will unfold another world". And so it was, day after day the serene face of the Buddha and the compelling beauty of the figures of Bhuvaneswar and Khajuraho revealed to me this other world far away from the figures of Athena and Apollo.

"After completing studies there and appearing in the preliminary examinations for Ph.D. I was at cross-roads. Do I pursue Western art, anesthetics, English and American literature or was there something else? Also in America one was called upon to speak on India. Although I did so I became deeply conscious of my ignorance about my own country and its people. I could have devoted my entire life in pursuing English literature and Western Arts and was keenly interested in them. I was equally intensely conscious of my ignorance in regard to India. This soon overpowered me. I was on a four year coveted fellowship for which only a few Asians were invited from entire Asia. I abandoned the fellowship after two years due to this restlessness. In those days few Indians would do that. US was the golden land of opportunities. My teachers in USA all fond of me wanted me to stay. I told them that I was deeply grateful to them. They had broadened my outlook and given me rare analytical skills. Nevertheless my calling now was to return to the land of my birth and explore the depths of its ancient culture. After my return, I continued to teach English. I taught at the Delhi University for five years. The urge to explore Indian tradition called for many efforts. One was to travel South, the other to rigorously pursue training in dance and music. I walked from Madurai to Kanyakumari and from Kanyakumari to Palghat".

On my inquiring whether she travelled all alone, she added, "No, we were three-four of us. One was a friend from Tamil Nadu. She continues to teach at Cambridge, another was a friend who had studied psychology in Freud School. He too returned to London. All of us had studied abroad and felt that we did not know our country."

I interjected, "Your working with renowned intellectuals as I.A. Richards and those connected with Freud School is really thrilling". But she went on in her stride, "Well yes. Although both I.A. Richards and Freud were important, we were seeking something different. This journey was extremely significant for me. I wrote a book on it. After that I went to Dr. Vasudev Sharan Aggarwal. He explained to me that while my curiosity and enthusiasm for Indian culture was well taken, it required systematic study and discipline. One had to begin from the beginning. Mere enthusiasm was not enough. Fortunately Acharya Hazari Prasad Dwivedi and Shri Rai Krishnadasa were at Benaras. They were family friends, so was Dr. Vasudeva Sharan Agrawal. I sought admission for Ph.D. programme at Benaras Hindu University. My entire background in English literature was a hindrance in acquiring admission. I had to appear for a Sanskṛit examination and only then was admission granted. Dr. Vasudev Sharanji had come to Benaras only sometime back. I was his first Ph.D. student. He laboured hard on me and kept me in strict discipline. I believe that what he invested in me far surpassed that in anybody else. I was fortunate to receive guidance and affection from Vasudeva Sharanji, Hazari Prasadji, Rai Krishnadasaji, Rajbali Pandeji, Kaviraj Gopinathji, Moti Chandraji and many other leading intellectuals. I stayed in the house of Premchandji. Shivraniji occupied the portion upstairs.

"I have expressed all this because it is the story of up-bringing and not one of career."

I clarified, "My basic curiosity has been regarding the major turn in your journey, the one towards the study of Indian Arts. Did the inspiration come from within, from the upbringing or from the compulsions of career. Your response has clarified that the transformation was motivated from inner forces and strong commitments? What was the topic of your research of the Indian arts and what was the language of your work?"

She replied, "English, the topic and the story of its selection is unique. These days, you know, a student enters the University and declares that he wants to do a Ph.D. He then looks for a subject. In my case, the subject gripped me, not Ph.D. I took up Ph.D. programme because Vasudev Sharanji said to me, 'You need discipline and control. Ph.D. will bring this'. The subject had already overpowered me. Having been trained in dance by noted 'Gurus', dance played an important role in the vision that I acquired after my return from America. When I travelled southwards and met Dr. Raghavan and Rukmini Arundale, and many other great scholars, I was convinced that the culture of this country is founded upon notions of holism and holistic perspective and that my practical education in dance was only a fragment of it. After meeting the textualists I realised that though great and deep in their knowledge, they were also fragmented because those well-versed with the texts (*shāśtra*) did not know about practice (*prayōga*). Those who knew the language and literature were often not responsive to the dimension of creativity. Those who knew creativity did not know the *shāśtra.* Those who knew literature were ignorant about music. Those who were competent in music did not know about dance. Those who knew dance were not concerned with literature, and the cultural context of their art. In short, there were many illuminated mirrors of a great tradition, nevertheless they were all parts of a holistic tradition which now lay fragmented. A reconstitution of the whole was necessary. This I believe happened primarily after the 19th century. There are many reasons about which I have written separately. That is why I chose the topic 'Inter-relationship of the Indian Arts' with dance at the center. How its image and symbolic dimension was and is pervasive from the vedas to the medieval literature? What is its position? On the other hand how are Indian architecture, sculpture and literature inter-related? Only a small portion of my first book *Classical Indian Dance in Literature and the Arts* contains my findings. The treatise was voluminous. Vasudeva Sharanji and Hazari Prasadji said that this girl has brought in three-donkey-loads of material. They were encouraging and thrilled. I was gratified now as they had been severe and critical during the apprenticeship. For me these years in Benaras are of great value.

"In this context, a dialogue between a king and Markandeya drawn from the 3rd section of the *Vishnudharmottara Purāna* is relevant. The King requested the sage, 'Kindly teach me the technique of worship'. The sage said, 'For that you need an idol.' The King said, 'I will make an idol myself. Teach me the art of sculpture.' The sage said, 'Before learning to sculpt images you should learn dance.' When the King agreed to learn dance, the sage said that before dance you must learn music. When the King learnt music, the sage asked 'Have you acquired competence in rhythm etc.' This is a long sequence as is common in our *purānas*. They begin with sculpture and reach out to rhythm. There are other stories. It would appear that this holistic perspective and framework of interdependence and inter-relatedness of different domains of life and of the arts was primary. While autonomy of genres and genus was recognised, the inter-dependence and mutual interpenetration was equally important. In course of time, and this is a complicated history, holistic perspective was fractured. It eventually led to self-centredness of each art form. Till few years back, autonomy of the arts was much talked about.

"My work operates at two levels. One is at the level of vision and the other of content and form. I have attempted modestly to explore this at the level of theory (*Sāstra*) as also creativity and experience. As you know, the concept of *rasa* embraces all arts. Until the artist subscribed to the primacy of the *rasa* principle, this inter-relatedness remained alive and vibrant. Also in the 19th century, however, due to influences from the West as also other reasons, the arts became centred around the individual. Then, these relationship became brittle. *Rasa* demands impersonalisation or depersonalisation and intensity and ecstasy. There is no room for individual and personal emotion. The moment the individual "I" was placed centre-stage of the artistic creation, you encounter another world of disparate parts. No longer could the theory of *rasa* provide a fundamental as also over-arching unity. Earlier texts like the *Nātyaśāstra* and its commentaries incorporate all forms of arts. Indian architecture, painting, music, dance and theatre and literature and branches of the same tree. My work attempts to explicate each relationship, be it architecture, sculpture, literature, painting or dance. I have raised the issue of *rasa* in the context of regional forms of theatre, called the national Indian theatre forms. I have taken up the principle of *rasa* in literature, painting, and theatre and have delineated the fundamental principles governing the arts in my *The Square and the Circle of the Indian Arts.* I have sought to demonstrate the perspective, the vision emerging from study and research at the level of theory and practice, *sastra* and *prayoga.*"

I probed further, "As Nehru Fellow you explored the *Gita Govinda* which I think was a part of your Ph.D. work. Yet, I feel tempted to ask you why out of all the Sanskrit works you selected the *Gita Govinda*?"

She revealed, "Rangraji, there is a story to it too. No, *Gita Govinda* was not the subject of my Ph.D. thesis. Anyway, when I began to learn dance, I used to perform or do *abhinaya* on the *ashtapadis* of *Gita Govinda.* I have learnt and studied the four styles of dance, specially *Bharatanatyam, Kathak, Odissi* and *Manipuri* under the tutelage of renowned Gurus; *Kathak* from Achchan Maharaj, *Bharatanatyam* from Bharatam Narayana Swami and Smt. Lalitha, *Odissi* from Guru Surendra Kumar Jena and *Manipuri* from Guru Amobi Singh. When I learnt and performed these *ashtapadis* in different styles, I became conscious of the underlying unity. Thus, we did an experiment many many years ago. Three persons performed the same *ashtapadi.* Birju Bhaiya (now Birju Maharaj) in *Kathak*; Lalitha Shastri in *Bharatanatyam,* and I in *Manipuri.* Now when I see dancers doing similar experiments my memory goes back to these year of early fifties. I believe this was a novel experiment then. Each dancer performed in his or her own style. Then there was no room for comparisons. In fact this was the time only to assert unique identity of each style and school. I saw a single vision, a common verse of poetry and a wide spectrum of possibilities at the level of formal manifestation. I went deeper into the poetry of Jayadeva and found that there was an intrinsic relationship between the poetic word and its articulation and expression through the diverse arts and schools of music and dance. Also it was obvious that in both, literature and poetry, the poetic word and metaphor was important. That although the *sthayi bhāva* was unitary, the *vyabhicāri* and *Sancāri bhāva* were many. The principle of *rasa* became clear to me. To my mind while one stream of the Indian tradition is eternal, unchanging, the other is one in which there is movement and constant change flux. Then, I took up the dimension of unity and diversity in the Indian arts and inter-relationship in the arts through a single text. The *Gita Govinda* provided an extraordinary possibility of exploring this.

"My search was not one of literature student. It began on the basis of *prayōga*; from the perspective of *prayōga* and at the level of *prayōga*; I moved to poetry, music, painting and the ritual from practice. From the *prayōga* I moved to the text. Once I entered the text I realised that this short epic poem (*laghu mahākāvya*) moved concurrently at the sensuous and the spiritual plane. From the text I went into the innumerable translation of the poem in Indian and foreign languages. Eventually I began to search for original manuscripts. Once I entered this field, I realised that there were over three thousand manuscripts, written in nearly twenty scripts. They were spread all over India. Although S.K. De had identified nearly ten commentaries, I found that there were thirty or more commentaries, each interpreting the poem differently. Even more fascinating was the speed with which the poem spread from eastern India, Bengal or Orissa to Nepal, Gujarat, South India and else where. The poem had travelled within fifty years of its composition to Patan and was already being sung in the temples. It travelled to Kerala and began to be sung in the Guruvayoor temple. It became part and parcel of the Radha Kalyanam tradition in Tamil Nadu and Karnataka. It was essential in temple ritual in Andhra and of course there was the strong and vibrant tradition of singing in Puri and Navadvipa. So, text commentaries and the ritual and singing traditions had to be explored. Besides there were the several sets of miniature paintings from Gujarat, Rajasthan and the hills of Punjab and Himachal based on the Gita Govinda. Lastly there was the interpretation of the Gita Govinda in the classical schools of dance, *Kathakali, Bharatanatyam, Kuchipudi, Odissi, Kathak* and *Manipuri*. The field was vast. It was an ocean. I was staggered at the variety and richness of the material. My experience in *prayōga* was the beginning of a never ending journey into the Indian tradition."

Coming to the vast impact of this great work, I observed, "*Gita-Govinda* is a multi-dimensional work with tremendous aesthetic effect, vivid imagery, excellent *sura* and *tāla*, besides its deep-rooted religious philosophy and spiritual approach, which inspire the *sahridya* to transcend not only his body, but also the *mana*, *buddhi* and *ahaṅkāra*. These qualities are, to my mind, responsible for its remarkable impact on the development of the Indian arts. You have researched intensively as well as extensively into this great work and your finds have been widely applauded. Will you kindly throw some light on the intrinsic nature of this 'magnum opus' and its resultant impact?"

Delving deep into this work, she said, "Dr. Rangra, as I have mentioned earlier, *Gita-Govinda* is a remarkable creation. I think, it has come at the end of a very long and glorious history of Sanskrit literature. It was also the beginning of a new era. Dr. Suniti Kumar Chatterji has opined and I am not sure if I agree with him, 'It was perhaps originally written in *Apabhransha* and then translated into what we today recongise as Sanskrit'. You have rightly mentioned that it is a multi-dimensional work. It is a multi-meaning work, I would like to say because the capacity of the Sanskrit language for containing within a particular word so many different levels of meaning that the same word can be understood in so many different shades. If a single word can have many meanings, a cluster of words, metaphors etc. that the poet picks up, the word which is already loaded with multi-meanings and then puts it into a metaphor which opens up many more levels. This whole module of a multi-dimensional meanings, is given a colour, a live significance. It has a musical score, it has rhythm to it and it has a movement to it. What a man, more than a computer, Jayadeva was! I have tried it on a computer. It cannot take even half that the poet was thinking of. So I think while on one hand as you have mentioned, it is multidimensional, on the other side it is highly mystical—I would not call it religious as you have said. It is highly mystical in its import because it talks about the relationship of the human with the Divine. What does it say? It says that the human longs for the Divine and Divine is incomplete without the human. You will remember that in *Śrimad Bhāgawat* in the Dasham Skand, there is a vague kind of a notion about Radha that he goes away with a special Sakhi. It is also true that Radha appears in *Gāthasaptasati* but it is the poet Jayadeva who gives Radha flesh and blood as an independent character. Now at the philosophic and mystical level we have to understand that earlier Krishna is the principle of the one and the Gopis—the principle of one and the many—Jayadeva introduces into this principle, not negating the principle of the one and the many, the principle of the one and the one, to be distinguished quite clearly from the philosophic term called the *Dvaita.* Later we understand this as *bhedābheda*, that is, there is differentiation and there is no differentiation, that what we know as *Dvaitādvaita*. In the *Gita Govinda* Krishna pines, Krishna repents. No god repents, but here Krishna does repent that he has made a mistake. He goes to Radha and says *Padapallava-mudaram*, put your feet on my head. This is reciprocal relationship of the one and the one.

"The poem also moves at another level. It is also a relationship in which Radha is maturer of the two. But she has also to purify herself. She has to suffer. Suffering of what kind? Not the suffering you have in drama. Her suffering is because she has to give up her ego; negate herself, every time she looks to the sky. She must cover herself only with *neelalochaña* the blue of the sky. All these interpretations are at the surface level. The girdle, *Karghani* etc. what are these? These are the ornaments of the ego. She will get him only when she gives up these ornaments. She has to transcend them. So, the poem works on multiple levels. It is couched in a highly sensuous imagery that people at time call it a profane poem of highly sensuous poetry. This is its import. Why does he couch it thus? Because the Indian view is that the body is not flesh, the body is not a snare, to be denied. There is, of course, a notion of *tapas* it is instrument of purification. Also the body is the temple. It is a medium of transcendence. He talk of immanence and transcendence together. Therefore having read this poem for decades, I think, it is mist upon mist. I don't know what its intrinsic nature is. But I know, its essence is, the essence of that which is perennial in the human; it is the capacity of the human to transcend through the body to get to that spirituality."

I ventured another interpretation, "You have put very clearly what looked very hazy earlier. The duality and non-duality are two levels at which both Radha and Krishna interact. At the level of duality Radha becomes superior and, hence, attainable. And, there are moments, as you have mentioned, in this major work when the Divine, Krishna, descends to the level of body and seeks Radha. When Radha comes down from the level of eternity or say divinity, she seeks Krishna. And when both attain the level of divinity, both merge into each other in union and cease to be a duality. Would you like to comment on this contention?"

She listened with interest and replied, "You have articulated it clearly. This tantamounts to an interpretation. Let us look at the poem in another way. On the surface it moves simply. Two people meet somewhere and somewhere they are separated and do not meet. The poem then is all about their separation. She complains of his dancing away with other Gopis having left her and he complains of her having gone away and he is very sorry and then the *Sakhis* try to put them together and there is a meeting of the two, that is *Sambhoga* but mainly it is *Viyoga*. Now, I would like to make a slight amendment to what you said about descending from divinity. I think, we look at it in a manner in which the hierarchies themselves are broken down, because we think in terms of hierarchies. It does not mean that when Krishna descends to Radha, she represents flesh. No, Radha does not represent flesh at all. Flesh is out of it all. It is couched in a language of the senses and we have to make a distinction between the Indian idea of *indriya* and what the English language calls flesh or senses. These are two different concepts, totally different concepts. The Christian concept of profanity, sensuousness etc.— nothing of the kind here."

I drew her attention to another concept, "We have an ancient concept called *indriyātita*". She affirmed, "Exactly, it is through *indriya*, the senses, that we get to what is beyond the senses, the *indriyātita*. Therefore, the eternal principle, the one and the one principle, has to realise that the omniscience is all right with the many. He has to go through the experience of the many, and the one and the one, that is Radha. To fulfil the desire for merging with the other, he has to go through the experience of merging with many. Radha knows the principle of the one and the one, but is unable to accept the principle of the one and the many. She is jealous, she always has the fantasy of being with him, but she is not able to, because she has the ego, *ahañkāra*, of being superior to everyone. Hence, hindrance. So she has to get rid of her *ahañkāra*. The moment she get rid of that, she is in supplication and she with persuasion goes to him. But after what may be called physical consummation, the spiritual *Advaita*, they have to separate again. And as the last *ashtapadis* clearly elucidate they have two distinct roles. She is to get back as a principle of *Prithvi* and it is the *mañgala kalaśa*—no longer he uses the word *pinapayodhara*—this word is *mañgalakalaśa* now. It is a total transformation. No longer are they compared to something. *Chamar* with which they celebrate the union is the earth's whisk. From that moment of complete *advaita*, of knowing and the giving up of everything—her ornaments, now she is adorned with fulfilment. It is with this experience of fulfilment that she is once again the giver, and no longer a seeker, a separated principle of the other. Therefore, the richness is there. This could be understood as simply everybody seeing it and dancing it at the most physical level. In fact the two now symbolise the whole universe and in the universe these two become dateless, timeless, spaceless entities. This world of imagination is highly sacred."

To elicit Kapilaji's views on the ancient Indian theory of *rasa*, I asked, "The aesthetic theory of *rasa* propounded by our ancient *āchāryas* provides the basic approach to appreciate and interpret not only a literary work, but also all other artistic creations. You are known for your integral vision of the Indian art in all its manifestations. Do you think, the ancient theory of *rasa* holds good even in this age of advanced technology and, if not, what other approach would be effective?"

She elucidated, "The ancient theory of *rasa* as propounded by Bharata is embedded in the Upanisadic thought certainly provides a fundamental ground for understanding Indian arts without exception. This is how I would put it. Although the theory was propounded primarily for what is called *Nātya*, it never excluded the other arts as is clear from the *Nātyaśāstra*. I therefore think that *rasa* theory was the first enunciation of a theory of the arts. It was later that, as the interpretators and some of the commentators who belonged to the field of literature, *alañkārshaśtra*, the focus shifted to *alañkārs* who thought that it was restricted only to literature. This notion needs to be corrected. Everything that we know in terms of Bhama to Visvanath in literature is also a reflection of an integral vision of arts. The integral vision is not mine, it is Bharata's; it has come from that source. I have written a short book on *Nātyaśāstra*, published by the Sahitya Akademi, in which I have articulated some of these ideas. Therefore, this is a theory which is abstracting life into certain archetypical principles. It is abstracting life into rainbow colours. The diversity of the artistic media, the word in literature, the mass and volume in sculptures, the line and colour in paintings, sound and configuration in *svaras* and music, the making of the *aṇgas* and *ūpangas* in dance—all these are the methodologies through which certain states of being can be evoked. When communicated to a spectator or reader we call it *Rasotpatti*. These are all bridges. The emerging of the transcendental state is a state which is indistinguishable, in which all these bridges vanish. That is, the very implements are destroyed and we come back to the *indriyātīta*. The dialects of this is challenging. You employ vehicles and tools of senses, sense perceptions only to transcend them from differentiation. You move to non-differentiation.

"I think, this theory provided a unity. It provided a kind of dialogue amongst and in between the arts. The problem is not of the advanced technology. The problem is three divinities. Those divinities are from the West. The problem is of Freud, of Darwin, of Marx and the industrial revolution which placed the individual, the distinctive individual, at the centre of the universe and this brings us to renaissance vision. When it came to India, the attitude of the artist to the art, the attitude of the individual toward the society, the attitude of the individual in relation to the transcendental centres changed and we inherited that. You know better than I know that the first art on which it made an assault was literature. As long as literature, as long as the poet, not only Jayadeva even from Chandidas, Vidyapati and all that you find in the regional and medieval poets and Andals, Namavars and Alvars, in Mirabai, Suradasa and Jananesvara, there was no segmentation. The segmentation started only when we ignored the theory of *rasa*. We ignored it because of these influences that had come and which we internalised. First of all it affected literature and then the visual arts, like sculpture, painting etc. We began to think of objects and objectivity. Everything and everybody was outside us, most of all nature. Earlier nature was within us. Nature was what we were observing in the language of the 19th century called naturalistic painting. Maybe we will come back to that. There are voices in the West also. In the recent seminar we did with Kathleen Raine, it was realised that the West is looking for integration and is keenly looking both inward and Eastward".

Now, I took up another prominent work of Kapilaji and observed, "Your monumental work *The Square and the Circle of the Indian Arts* is a deep study of the ideational background of the Indian arts and the emergent principles of form. Will you kindly pinpoint for a layman like me, your conclusions of this rare study?"

She was modest as usual, "I don't know whether it is monumental and I don't know whether it is rare. But I think *The Square and the Circle of the Indian Arts* is the result of another insight I had into the Indian tradition. As I have told you, I had started my journey on the arts through practice, the practice of dance. Theory followed. I have quoted the *Vishṇudharmottara Purāna* many a time. Then came another stage and I will point at three levels. I realised that the Indian arts were not only a phenomenon of inter-relationship between and amongst the arts. Their foundations lay deep in domains we don't easily identify. First, when I was exposed to and also involved in, is *Karmakāñda* which one commonly understands as *yajña*. On the other, the fundamental principles of Indian mathematics. Third, that the Indian system of medicine viewed the body organism very differently than the Greeks. When this dawned upon me. I realised that Bharata in evolving this theory must have many antecedents. It could not just come out of the blue. We don't know even the place. Then I went far more deeply into the Vedic resources and the Upanisadic thought, because Bharata says at one point, 'I am going to devise and propound something from the *Nātya* and this is in a *yajña*.' Now, for anybody sitting in the 2nd century B.C./A.D. cannot use loose words for saying any thing. There must be some significance to it. There is sanctity, in using both the words *yajña* and *yōga*. Why did he use these words? Then I realised that one stream was the ideational, the speculative thought, and the focus again was on the senses and body as in our *Upanisads*. The second was the actual structure, this came from the *yajña* like the *agnichayana* etc. Bharata had a kind of code that we know in the medieval Hindi poetry as *ulatbasi* i.e. you say something, while you mean something else.

"What this book *The Square and the Circle of the Indian Arts* seeks to do is to identify the sources which may have been the Pre-Bharata resources and how they affect emergence of a theory of art. The *Upanisads* have a very definite approach to the whole world, which is clearly articulated not in the Vedanta philosophy but the early *Upanisads*. For me the *Chhandogyopanisad*, the *Kathopanisad*, the *Taittiriyopanisad* are very important *Upanisads* in which the relationship of senses the body, the mind and the soul is articulated. The relationship of man and the nature, of *ātmā* and *brahman* and of the *vyakta* and *avyakta* is articulated. Also the relationship between *jivātma* and *paramātma*, although these words have not been used, is articulated. Instead, the words *piṇda* (micro) and *brahmanda* (macro) are used. That is one level. There is another stream which can be identified with *Brāhmans* with *Yajurveda* as the fountain head particularly the *Satpatha Brāhmana* in which the details of a *yajña* of seven to twenty-one days are described. All the altars have a significance. There are five layers of *chiṭṭi* in the *yajña*, five types of offerings are prescribed which are symbolic of five senses. Then, the fire rituals which we had considered as mere formalities, are instead the methodology of replicating the cosmos. The world is made and unmade in that duration. Each of the three altars signify different type of space and are made in different shapes. The celestial altar is in the form of a square. The terrestrial fire is a circle. The domestic fire is a semicircle. Thus, there is the employment of basic geometrical forms.

"Now the question is how the ideational background and the structure is reflected in the arts? When I reflected it was clear that the same principles governed the Indian arts. It all begins with a point (*bindū*) and then a circle and square is drawn. Horizontals, verticals and diagonals are drawn. Each of these lines has an emotive value, the *trivikrams*, symbolises three steps. The moment you draw a diagonal it is that which tells you of *trivikrams*. The diagonal is an *urdhvarekha*. All these are the elements of form. There is the basic geometry to it *silpa panjara*. Then there is *Nātya Purusha*. In music we have the *Sangita Purusha*. Then each of the senses and each of the elements are in the *chakrās* of the body. If you differentiate the sounds, each sound has an emotive value, a particular note, is related to day and time. It is a complex, a tight book, but I think it has laid the foundation of much greater and deeper study of how to approach the Indian arts. We have to ignore the minor happenings and look at the basic grand design of our arts".

I raised another relevant point, "Is Patanjali's *Yoga Sutra* in anyway related to our arts? Has it contributed in any way to their evolution?"

She confirmed, "Patanjali is every important. The *Yoga Sutra* not only takes into account but also permeates the thinking and expression modes of all our arts. This work is of great relevance. The emphasis of the body, mind and soul is the crux of both the *yogasūtra* and the *rasa* theory understandability; the theory of *rasa* is interpreted in terms of all the six schools of the Indian philosophy, the *saddarshanas*."

Touching another aspect of practising the arts, I remarked, "Pursuit of all arts is called *Sādhanā* and many artists compare the creative act with that of meditational *yōga*. Being a creative as well as the performing artists yourself, you must have gone through the wonderful experience many a time. Would you like to share your experience with us?"

Welcoming the question, she said, "Dr. Rangra, I can speak only about one part of your question. Yes, as I have said in my earlier writings on the Indian arts, it is a *yōga*, a *sādhanā* and also in terms of Gita, *Karmsu Kaushalam*. You may call concentrated work a *sādhanā*. It can be through any medium. The scientist, the poet, the philosopher, the potter, the maker of images—all do a *sādhanā*. As a student of literature you know Wordsworth made a statement that poetry is the spontaneous outburst of powerful feelings. Eliot instead spoke of impersonalisation and depersonalisation. I believe that while poetry may appear as spontaneous overflow of powerful emotions, this can only happen when the small or lower self has been conquered or certainly subjugated. Poetry or any art cannot be uplifting if all they communicate is the creator poet's, subjectivity. It is only when you have transcended subjectivity that there can be creativity. As you know, the difference between a poetry and a lesser form of poetry. In the former experience one is able to uplift oneself beyond this self. It is the poetry that remains and not the person. You know that already and you have written about it. Similarly in the case of musician you don't see the musician singing, you hear the music and do not concentrate on the person through whom you hear the music. You don't see the dancers, you see the dance. It is *yōga* because it is a discipline. This is contrary to the popular notion that the artist is an indisciplined person. Instead, it is only the disciplined artist who has the freedom to be an artist. It is the artist who is the most disciplined person. For him discipline is first and foremost and even has it in selecting his own emotions.

"I am not a creative artist. I can only say that I have many creative artists as my teachers and I have lived with many artists. What is creative and what is not, is also a different question? It is a relative question. How can I tell you that there were moments of both in the actual experience of the dance, both as a dancer and also in seeing dance or listening to poetry, as I would put it, of absolute ecstasy. These moments are the most indescribable moments. I asked a question last year to a computer person, since now they have artificial intelligence in which everything can be measured. As a dancer I asked him that I danced the same thing, everyday perhaps, sixty times. One day the person who sings knows that something happened. I also know it happened. Will the machine be able to tell the difference in what happened to my metabolism etc. The answer was that to know that we will have to put so many nodes on you. I said, 'The moment you put on nodes on me, I am no longer a free person'. So what it is and what is not in the realm of discursive thought at all. So what is not in this realm, we should respect it."

Kapila Vatsyayan has organised remarkable seminars and exhibitions on highly subtle but basic concepts of Indian arts which prompted me to observe,"The unforgettable seminars and exhibitions on *Ākāśa*, *Ākāra*, *Kāla*. *Prakrti*, *Ṛta-Ṛtu* visualised and organised by you, have done a great service to the Indian art and culture, besides enlightening the modern mind on these subtle concepts. Shall we expect more seminars and exhibitions on such basic concepts?"

Touching the background of this magnificent effort, she said,"What I have done in the seminars and exhibitions in visualising these, is a clear extension of the kind of work and insight we were talking about earlier. All my research brought me to the primary concepts which were guiding the Indian arts, the Indian world view. This I believe could be extended to other civilisations and cultures. So I took on certain perennial universals and the different type of globalisations which have brought the world together over a long span of history. The sciences and the humanities, the theory and the practice, Medicine and Geology, Botany and flora and fauna and all that what it is after all if not Space, (*Ākāśa*). The idea of Space and Time, are the two basic concepts, which are at the root of all the makings of nations, cultures. Inner space and outer space, the notions of time, *Ākāśa*, *Kāla* and *Ākāra* are related. This was followed by discussions on the five primal elements i.e. *Prithvi*, *Agni*, *Jal*, *Vāyu* and *Ākāśa*. Some cultures have five primal elements and some have four like the Chinese. There are differences, of course. Then the idea of a cosmic order and chaos *Ṛta* and *Anrita*. Now, Physics and Astrophysics are asking these questions. These questions have already been asked by *Upnisads*, the makers of the Chinese civilisation, Mayan and Greeks. This is the world we live in which has determined civilisational modes, perspections and value systems. The notion of the mere economic man is shrinking the concept of the human being to a mere limited material entity of ephemeral significance.

"I have completed in these last ten years the first round, the first cycle. This has taken into account space, time, primal man, elements and the concepts of eco-balances and then *Ṛta*, chaos and order. These theme are much discussed in modern Physics and relevant in the context of the debate on self organising systems.

"This year we start another concentric circle. This time we want to put the mind of man in the centre and, I think, there will be another series in the next few years."

I asked, "Does it mean that from *Brahmāṇda* you will now come to *Pinda*?" she affirmed, "That's right, the first thing would be Man, Mind and the Mask".

Winding up the discussion, I put a very personal and introspective question, "You have continued all along with two parallel vocations—one of Advisor, an Institute builder, an administrator, and the other of a creative and performing artist as well as a relentless researcher. You must have found many a time one picking up a row with the other, disturbing your inner peace and concentration. How do you manage to bring about a thaw between the two for the success of your mission?"

She admitted frankly, "Dr. Rangra, you know, there is always a *Mahābhārat* going on inside one's physical being, *Kāyā* and cells fighting with one another. So much is going on inside that I don't even know how much is going on. But the microbiologist tells me that there is a constant movement and I am not what I was talking to you five minutes ago. All that comes together in terms of what is identifiable in the sense what can be seen on the outside.

"Yes you are right, from the early days I had two callings. One was my critical calling, not only doing English literature, but also my other and myself. In fact there were very many selves. I have really been fortunate in certainly having sometimes a conflict on how much time to be spent on one thing. But at the conceptual level, at the inner level, there was no conflict as I tried to look at it like this. If I had been only an administrator I would have been working in an Economic Ministry—I did once appear in the civil service examination which I did not finish and I might have been a Custom Collector or something. But I am not that. I have been involved in advising. That is why I joined the Ministry of Education from the University because I wanted to transform the Indian education system—one did not succeed in doing. But then in the field of the Indian languages, Hindi and Sanskrit I have been able to do something. There was also a question of ensuring parity of pay-scales of those who were in Sanskrit and others in the Museums, Archaeology, the Akademis, the Centre for Higher Tibetan Studies—all this has given me great satisfaction. This brought me in touch with the domain of knowledge which sitting as a mere researcher I might not have got. Then also I kept my research work going on. If I had not the opportunities of both, the experience in the flow of the tradition—the musicians, the dancers, the painters, the poets craftsmen—and if I had not the critical insight into the theory and if I had not the opportunity for observing others as in-charge of international cultural relations, I could not have accomplished the little I have.

"Yes, there is a problem. The problem is not of a conflict between whether this calls me more or the other. The problem is that of the physical time and I wish I had all the twenty-four hours for each of these pursuits. Then I would have been very happy. But I have to pull myself out of something I am fully involved in order to find time for something which pulls me equally. For instance, I am involved in dancing and don't want to go to a meeting. I want to make the blue print of an institution, but I am called elsewhere. So I feel divided in term of the physical time. Thus, it is mainly a question of organisation of the physical time therefor, I take these pendulum, I devote myself heart and soul to one and then switch over to another, as in the case of the Nehru Fellowship. That time was so great and meaningful for me. I hope, I can do that again."

(New Delhi—21.2.1997)

*

Mannu Bhandari

B. 3.4.1931, Bhanpura, Madhya Pradesh; *mt.* Hindi, *edn.* M.A.; *car.* Former Reader, Miranda House, Delhi Uni., now writing; *pubs. short story collections* Hār Gayī, Teen Nigahon Kī Ek Tasvīr, Ek Plate Sailāb, Yahī Sach Hai, Trishanku, Merī Priya Kahāniyān, Das Pratinidhi Kahāniyān; *novels* Ek Inch Muskān (in collaboration), Āpkā Bantī, Mahābhoj; Swāmī *play* Binā Dīvāron Ke Ghar; many successful stage presentations of Mahābhoj; a film Rajnigandhā based on Yahī Sach Hai; filming of Swamī; her writings translated into many Indian languages.

Inner Recesses of Creativity

To live a fragmented life at various levels is the destiny of the modern woman. In an attempt to strike a balance between ambitions of her own and those of her close relation she undergoes a great deal of stress and strain that takes her to a breaking point again and again. The desire to move out of the four walls of the household to achieve something worthwhile ushers her into a fierce battle of attrition which complicates her life more and more. But the greatest struggle that she has to carry on incessantly is against her own tradition-bound 'sanskars' pitched within which often come in her way. Ever since marriage assumed the stature of a compromise, slipping from the padestal of a religious institution, the relationship of husband and wife and its stability has suffered immensely. Their inflated egos, real or imagined, intrusion by an outsider, take no time to wreck it. Divorce and remarriage are no more looked upon as unseemly incidents, though their worst consequences are to be borne by the off-spring.

An intensive, psychological and in-depth portrayal of all these and many more subtle and terrible problems faced by the modern woman are found in Mannu Bhandari's fiction. She occupies a prominent place among the modern Hindi fiction writers. Spontaneity is the hallmark of her writings. The simple and direct linguistic pattern of her works catches the mind of the readers and sways them. There is no artificiality or craftiness, for everything, seems to be just effortless. She has published many short story collections but the ones like *Yahī Sach Hai* (this is the truth), *Mein Hār Gayī* (I am defeated), *Oonchayi* (Height), *Ek Plate Sailab* (One Plate of Flood), *Ek Bar Aur* (Once more), *Keel aur Kasak* (Nail and Stinging Pain), were highly applauded and evoked multiple reactions. Her novel *Āpkā Bantī*

(Your Banti) has acquired the status of a classic. Keeping the boy Banti at the centre, this work presents a heart-rending analysis of the inner and outer conflicts of the modern woman trying to preserve an individuality of her own, forced to live a fragmented life at various mental and social levels because of her inter-action with her alienated husband and a young son who grows up under utter confusion. Her other novels are *Mahabhoj* (A Grand Feast) and *Swami* (Master). *Mahabhoj* is a pungent satire on the politics of votes and *Swami* being the modern version of Sarat's famous character Saudamini. *Yahi Sach Hai* and *Swami* were filmed, whereas *Mahabhoj* was successfully staged many a time.

Mannu Bhandari is simple by nature, least conscious of her achievements. When I got an opportunity to discuss her own writings with her, this trait of her personality opened up many dimensions of her creativity as also its inner recesses. Initiating the discussion I asked, "You must have picked up many of your characters from real life. Did you ever feel in the course of your creative act that you are nearing the truth, transcending your earlier experience? If so, please relate your inner experiences in creating Banti, Shakun or Da Sahib."

Recollecting for a while and searching within, she replied, "No doubt most of my characters have come from real life. But their forms as they took in my works are so different from those in real life that it is almost difficult to correlate them. In fact, no author would ever aim at reproducing those in real life.

"So far as I am concerned, when any person or incident clicks, I am not able to write on it immediately. I either store it in a corner of my mind or note it in my diary. Later when I feel like according a meaning to some incident or underlining some problem or person or lending a meaningful extension or depth to the personality of a character, a person or an incident emerges from the store-house of my mind. Then with a proper blending of both, a story or novel is born.

But in this process neither the person nor the incident retain their origin form. It so happens many a time that characters lying in the store house of my mind are not able to take a form for want of favourable environment. Sometimes incidents also lay unused for want of suitable characters. If it could be found out, in the mind of any writer many incidents and characters would be lying in waiting for taking the shape of a worthwhile story or novel".

When I asked her to elucidate in the context of a particular character from her fiction, she observed, "It is rather difficult, and strenuous too, for me to meet your demand for elaborating my creative process, specifically with reference to any of my prominent characters such as Da Sahib, Banti or Shakun. I may, however, try. Banti and Shakun are the central characters of the novel. Ajay remains only in the background. In real life I met Shakun for just an hour and even that was a very formal meeting. I saw Banti too only for ten minutes, just saw him, that is all. My real acquaintance was with Ajay. But after Shakun's remarriage when Ajay insisted on, rather took a unilateral decision, to take Banti with him, only Banti and Shakun got registered in some corner of my mind. I was shaken by one thing only—that a child remaining with his mother right from the birth will be separated just on the insistence of his father and that too at a tender age when he needs his mother's company the most. Later, one or two families in my knowledge had to face a similar problem, though in a different context and situation. Later, when all these situations, started taking the form of a social problem, the real Banti and Shakun went into oblivion. A new Banti and Shakun were born, new situations got created which on one hand threw light on the fallacy of inter-relationship between child and parents and on the other underlined a complex social dilemma. All I wish to emphasise is that the role of the original incident and character was not in any case more than a drop in an ocean, but a drop that formed the very basis of the whole novel".

Probing further, when I urged her to throw some light on the emergence of Da Sahib in her novel *Mahabhoj*, she quipped, "You seem to be enamoured of the Janmapatri (birth chart) of fictional characters. Anyhow Da Sahib was a very pleasant, courteous and soft spoken person, a highly respected and honoured active freedom fighter of the city. I was acquainted with him as he often came to meet my father, but the direct encounter happened in July, 1947.

"The struggle for freedom was at its climax in 1946-47 and fervour of the students soared up skyward. I was not only participating in the movement to the best of my ability, but was also cast in the role of a leader. Consequently, some of us were debarred from admission. The whole dispute was based on this and all the students of the college were with us. It became a major issue. After inviting the Director of Education from Delhi we had enough strength on our side. Then came Da Sahib to mediate. The way he assured us that he will compel the college authorities to concede to our genuine demands, we were fully satisfied. So we relented but then he ditched us in the nick of time and we fell flat on our back. It is a long story. To be brief, the double-face of this man shook me to my roots at the tender age of sixteen. These days everybody is double-faceted in politics, but that was an age of idealism, and that was why we were too shocked. However, time is the best healer and we forgot everything. After full thirty-one years when the theme of *Mahabhoj* began taking shape with the visualisation of the main characters of the novel, that very Da Sahib came to life again in the form of the hero. Then, many dimensions of his personality came to light in the changed circumstances. It was a matter of surprise for me and also of satisfaction".

Her novel *Apka Banti* became a classic in no time. When the conflicting egos of a married couple seeking self-gratification cross the boundaries of verbal duals and enter the realm of divorce, their children are bound to suffer immensely. The situation becomes worse when the mother on whom falls the responsibility of rearing the children, remarries. This is exactly what happened with Banti when his mother Shakun remarried. The author rightly observes in the 'Janma-patri of 'Banti' (The Birth chart of Banti), 'I think, I do not consider either Shakun or Ajay wrong, Banti is also not wrong at all. What can be turned right or wrong are the mutual relationship of Ajay-Shakun and Banti. But the irony of the entire situation is that the person least responsible for all this and the most innocent of them all, that is Banti, has to suffer the most in this tragedy'.

Yet, recollecting my reaction to the above observation I asked Mannuji, "To find out factors leading to this irony you had to delve deep into the psyche of Shakun since Ajay was present only in his absence. If despite your efforts to build up Banti, the centre of your attention had been Shakun throughout, what was wrong in it? Perhaps, you have tried to negate this in the 'Janmapatri'. But why?"

She replied, "So far as I think, I have never negated the importance of Shakun. All that I have negated is her being the central character. Even today I am absolutely clear that Banti is the central character of the novel. Of course, Shakun is at the centre of Banti's life. Banti lives with her. His happiness and sorrows are linked with her. Banti is at the receiving end of the consequences of all her actions and decisions. In a way, Shakun is the regulatory character of Banty's life, but it is not essential that the regulatory character should also be the central character. The whole novel is concentrated on the eight years old, Banti. In the beginning, Banti has his 'own' house, his 'own' garden, his 'own' mother, his 'own' aunt. Though Papa does not live with him, he loves Banti beyond limit. Banti has in his possession a heap of toys given by Papa. But within a year how all these things left him one by one. He lost his aunt, lost his house, lost his mother, and Papa also ceased to be as he was before. In other words, the child living under deep and warm relationships became relationless, all the ties got snapped. The novel ends with this line 'Even Papa's face merged with those of the aliens', that is, even the last contact disappeared. My aim in the novel was to depict in all its dimensions, Banti's journey of becoming gradually rootless and I have concentrated mainly on Banti."

Provoking her further, I asked, "Did you have another encounter with the real Banti or Shakun?" She replied in the negative, "No, I don't know even how the real Banti or Shakun faced the whole situation, or what happened to them. But the Banti and Shakun who got evolved as a result of their own actions-reactions to the situations created by me, are entirely different from the original ones. Ordinarily the women in our society live under family ties which form the very basis of their evaluation—an ideal daughter, ideal wife, ideal sister or ideal mother; whether transcending these relationships, she could have a independent personality, any desires and ambitions of her own, any dreams of her future life, is considered irrelevant. It never occurred to any one to recognise or accept her, as an individual. But whenever she rose to fulfil her personal ambitions, she was questioned. She was questioned both from within and without, falling a prey to her inhibiting *Sanskars* dating back to centuries. Look at Shakun; she is the principal of a college, has not only her own independent personality but also respect in the society. When under the advice of the Vakil uncle and after marrying Dr. Joshi she plans her future, Banti not only rejects this very idea, but also starts a full-length rebellion against her. This splits Shakun's personality into two—inner conflicts between her role as a mother and as a woman. When her motherhood awakens, she suffers intensely with the sense of guilt for being cruel and unjust to Banti. She cries helplessly. But when the womanhood awakens in her, she is annoyed with Banti's reactions. When all her efforts to please Banti fail, she decides to send him to Ajay, though after sending Banti away, she spends not a single day in peace. Above all, she suffers from a sense of guilt. Right from the beginning the untold dimensions and layers of Shakun's personality get revealed gradually and I consider this my success, besides the sense of satisfaction".

Touching upon the subject of staging and filming of her writings, I observed, "Some of your writings have been staged as well as filmed. Do you adapt them yourself for these media or you leave this work to others? Were you satisfied with their production? In the event of dissatisfaction how do you react to them, besides being left with no option except to putting up with the 'liberty taken by others".

She replied, "I adapted some of them myself, leaving the remaining ones to others, but the success of staging or filming does not depend on the adaptation alone. The stage-adaption of *Mahabhoj* was prepared by myself in cooperation with director Amal Alana, after putting in a lot of hard work. Believe me, it took me full eight months. It was a successful and forceful production. But I have seen many weak productions based on this very script. In fact, the success of this medium depends upon the whole team. Direction, acting, light scheme, music, stage-craft, their right coordination and their collective impact, everything counts to make it a success. The script has its own importance undoubtedly as it prepares the background, but without the cooperation of all these, things do not come to a successful culmination."

"Now, coming to putting up with the liberty taken by others, one has to endure it even in the case of translation. It appears to you as if by translating a thing into another language, the very life has run out of the original, while the form of both is similar, whereas staging and filming is a different media altogether, from audio to visual. Hence change is a must with them. However, by way of caution, it must be ensured that the writing is entrusted to the right director. Though the success of these media depends upon the entire team, yet these are mainly the media of the director. But how many writers are fortunate enough to choose the director?"

Mannu Bhandari's novel *Swami* was inspired by Sarat's story with the same title. The introduction of the novel reveals that Basu Chatterji wanted to base a film on this story of Sarat and on his request Mannu re-wrote the story as Basu was not satisfied with its present form. The introduction also indicates that by recasting the heroine Saudamini in the new form she converted the original story of self-pity coupled with the sense of guilt, to that of a simple humanitarian inner conflict. Towards the end of the introduction she feels sorry for Sarat reinterpreting his story. With this background, I asked her, "May be on the request of Basu Da, you 'raped' Sarat's story *Swami* to re-cast his heroine Saudamini into your own mould. But towards the end of the story Basu Da by making her fall at the feet of her husband reverted her to Sarat's mould. Thus, you were left with nothing but regret. The writer in Sarat's soul must be cursing you."

Refuting my charge, she replied, "Neither I accept the charge that I indulged in any sort of high-handedness with Sarat's story, nor do I agree with the contention that by making Saudamini fall at her husband's feet Basu reverted this story to Sarat's point of view. The chart of action-reaction of events relating to her husband as formed in the story conform to my story precisely. Starting from sheer neglect he develops compassion, affection, regard and respect gradually. In a way the journey symbolises a march from non-believing to believing. My difference with Basu Da was only on making her fall at her husband's feet which I came to know only while viewing the film. Then, I discussed with him at length and learnt that the twist he gave at the end was inspired neither by the intention to return the story to Sarat, nor was it done under the pressure of the public taste. It was in fact the urge of the feudal *Sanskar* that has taken roots in the Indian psyche which is satisfied only when a woman falls at a man's feet. Ninety percent of our men folk suffer from this complex in one form or the other.

"Anyhow, except this ending, *Swami* is a good film, not in my won opinion but in the opinion of other viewers also, and therefore, the idea of regret never came to my mind."

Later during an exclusive session on her short stories, I observed, "Many of your short stories haunt your readers. I have myself struggled for years with your stories like *Yehi Sach Hai* (This is the truth) and *Oonchayi* (Height) though I came to my own conclusion that these stories highlight the trend of a detached self-indulgence. This may be a lopsided view. So I seek your elucidation."

She threw a counter question at me, instead of replying to my question, "I can admit this view in regard to the story *Yehi Sach Hai*. But why did *Oonchayi* haunt you?" I observed, "It is the shamelessness of its heroine that haunted me. When her extra-marital affair is exposed, her distressed husband asks, 'Well Shiboo, tell me whether you never thought of me even once at that time?' she replied with exemplary warmth, 'You talk of thought. There was none except you in my mind. Though he had ridden my body, it was only you who were occupying my mind.' Then, she stops for a while and adds, 'The place that you have in my life, nobody else can even grab it. Leave aside grabbing none can even touch it. I may be available to anybody and to any extent, may even indulge in physical affairs, but the height at which you are set in my mind, nobody can ever measure up to that.' Don't you think that all the prevalent concepts of love will fall flat before this 'height'? I think, this applies to the story *Yehi Sach Hai* also."

Picking up the end of my observation, she remarked, "The heroine of *Yehi Sach Hai* is attracted to both the heroes equally. Her problem is that she is not able to accept this fact as she has imbibed from the very beginning the *sanskar* that it is appropriate, and ethical too, to love only one person at a time. So when she is with one lover she negates her love for the other, and when she is with the second lover, she considers her love with the first one as an adolescent infatuation. But later when she is again with the first one and the same old tender feeling towards him comes up, she justifies it to herself that the first love was the true love, the second love being just a space-filler. I have tried to depict this inner emotional conflict of a girl with an impartial approach. This story, written thirty-five years back, was highly applauded for the boldness with which a female writer honestly depicted the split-personality of a young girl. It must have haunted you also for the reason that you could not accept the plausibility of a girl's love divided between the two boys at a time".

In my question I had referred to her short story *Oonchayi* also. So, coming to that she observed, "This story was inspired by a quotation which reads: 'Real love is so pure, so high that minor infidelities do not matter'. I based the story on this and it was much talked about. But later it dawned upon me that this story was a sort of imposition—a false story which no husband would ever accept. This story could startle the readers, could also keep them wondering but it could not touch their heart, since it is not a slice of real life. I realised later that though the story contained fine, well-chiselled dialogues and high flown idioms, it missed the very throb of life. How could a husband verify that his wife's statements were true? How could he accept them on their face value? No husband would ever accept it as true".

I probed further with reference to her short story *Yehi Sach Hai*, "A collection of your short stories *Das Pratinidhi Kahāniyan* (Ten representative Short Stories), published by Kitabghar recently, does not contain this story. Does it mean that the 'truth' expressed in the story remains no more true in your view now and that you are still attached to the contention that real love is directed to one person only, not two?"

She replied, "For this collection, I selected only those stories of mine which represented fully my thoughts, beliefs and convictions and it is a fact that *Yehi Sach Hai* cannot be counted among these. But that does not mean that its truth ceases to be my truth now. Honestly speaking, that was not my truth even then. I used to find myself then in an unending discussion to the extent of a dispute with a friend who was suffering from the agony of being split between the two. Whether there is anything like true love, I don't know, but it is true that whatever goes by the name of love cannot bear division, a duality. To have a love affair with two is neither love nor infatuation, it is rather a deceit.

"Despite this belief, I wrote the story. I identified myself with the split-mind and dilemma of my friend to such an extent that I wrote the story in first person, and adopted the diary style to make it a document of personal experience. But since I was not one with the idea of having an affair with two, the heroine when in the company of one, never fails to negate the other. On coming in contact with the second lover she negate the first by alleging that the love indulged at the age of sixteen is no love, but sheer adolescent sentimentality. But when she meets the first, she negates the second apologetically saying, 'first love is the true love. You filled the gap in its absence. You were a complement, but I took you as the dearest', I don't remember precisely, but such were the statements she made. That is, despite her attraction to both, she did not accept it and negated them. It was this negation perhaps that implied my personal belief, my own truth."

My next question was a bit personal. I remarked, "Some people believe that every piece of fiction is more or less autobiographical. From this point of view, which one of your writing you find closest to you?"

She told me at the outset that she could be found the most in her story *Trishanku* (Hung). Then delving deep into my question, she observed, "The author is, no doubt, present in his writing somewhere, but this presence need not be the part of his autobiography. It is neither essential nor possible. How many writings can a writer squeeze out by concentrating on his own life each time? That way he would either run out completely or start repeating himself. But if the area of his experiences is vast, wide and multidimensional, then it would be different. Otherwise, those with limited experiences like me, have to transcend their limits. No writer remains confined to the events of his personal life. His beliefs, his convictions and ambitions, his mental make up are also an integral part of his life and they are reflected in every writing in one way or the other. It is through them that he remains present in his writings. Any writer is inspired to write about by those characters, contents and intents which touch subconsciously his inner chords. It is perhaps for these reasons, I found myself nearest to Banti and Shakun, though my novel *Apka Banti* is not based on any event of my personal life. Similarly, Bisu and Binda of my novel *Mahabhoj* represent the repressed desire in me that there should at least be someone who is capable of raising his voice against injustice and exploitation. Thus, Mahesh of *Mahabhoj* represents my conviction and anger against the hollowness of bookish knowledge.

"It is true that while reading a short story or a novel one often thinks that much of it could be autobiographical. But the simple reason for this is that unless a writer identifies himself with the experience of other to the extent that they appear to be his own, he cannot write genuinely. It is the state of blending of self and otherness which lends each of his writings the image of being autobiographical."

My next probing was, "Writers remain generally attached to their earlier writings. You have also referred to such an attachment in your preface to your collection *Das Pratinidhi Kahaniyan*. Why do the early works of some writers happen to be their best writings? May be that experiences of life find spontaneous and honest expression with full gusto and in their true form in early writings, whereas on getting recognition a writer becomes less spontaneous and more self-conscious and practical. Would you like to comment?"

She contested my view, "I am not aware of any writer whose very first writing became his best writing. Experiences expressed in earlier writings could be honest and sincere, but it is not enough for being the best writing. To cast these experiences into excellent writings an artistic approach and fine craftsmanship is also required and these qualities are acquired gradually and with practice. It is true that the characters of my earlier short stories have impressed my mind immensely, but I don't consider them my best writings. Those are raw and unchiselled short stories which reveal the tendency to pour out more than the concerted effort to create. This is why I could write a full story in one sitting and the first draft with minor changes used to be the final form. But in my creative process as I became 'self-conscious' in your words, writing became difficult. You have used this word in a derogatory form, but I mean 'awareness'—more aware, more serious and more devoted to my work."

"Oh yes, it is also true that some writers of our generation and the earlier one, after giving their best works started pouring out second-rate weak stuff. But instead of linking this fact with any kind of practicality or cleverness, I would like to emphasise that keeping on writing without any inner pressure or urge must be the root cause of all this degeneration. Again, this is also neither necessary nor possible that all the writings of a writer should be or would be his best or the graph of his writings should go up from better to best."

Then, I took up the issue of a writer's fulfilment, "Which of your writings so far have give you creative satisfaction or fulfilments?" She kept quiet for a while and then overcoming her initial hesitation, she quipped, "It is rather difficult to attend to a question of this kind, yet if I must I would admit that it is *Apka Banti* and *Mahabhoj* among my novels and *Trishanku* amongst the short stories fall in this category."

Summing up the discussion, I observed, "The writer when he looks beyond his writings, feels like losing his faith in the power of the word and a sense of futility in writing sets in. Did it ever happen with you also?"

Weighing the implications of the question, she said, "In my life as a writer I have realised the limitation of the word many a time and at many levels. Words often fall short of expressing your sensations, but for this reason I never questioned the role of the word, Oh yes, I have been realising the futility of writing for some years past, but it is for reasons relating exclusively to our environment."

(New Delhi—8.7.1991 & 30.9.1995)

*

Kabita Sinha

B. 16.10.1931, Calcutta, *mt.* Bengali; *edn.* B.A., Dip. in Liby. Sc.; *car.* Former Director, Darbhanga Centre of A.I.R., now writing; *Awards & hons.* Līlā Award of Cal. Uni., 1976; *Pubs. poetry* Sahaj Sundarī, 1965, Saptādash Ashwārohi, 1974, Kabitā Parmeshwarī, 1976, *novels* Sonā Rupār Kāthī, 1956, Pāp-Punya Periye, 1964, Patner Biruddhe, Chār Jan Rāgi Jubatī, 1973, Ekati Kharāp Meyer Galp, 1973, Paurush, 1984; *Hindi edn.* Badnām Ladkī.

Woman: The First Rebel

Kabita Sinha has a prominent place among the women writers who came into the forefront in the post-Independence Bengali literature. She is known for her boldness, both in life and literature. She believes that a woman must be self-dependent. In her preface to the Hindi-edition of her novel *Ekti Khrāp Meyer Galp* (The Story of a Bad Girl) she remarks, "To expect any help or support from others is to entertain an illusion. Overcoming this temptation, I decided to fight my battles myself. I may not claim much success, but that did reveal to me my own strength." She asserts that woman is the first rebel of this universe. In her famous poem "Eve to God" she gives eloquent expression to this belief:

"I was the first
To touch
The tree of knowledge
I was the first
To realise
To live both in happiness and sorrow
In sin and virtue
Is remarkable
It was I
Who broke
The golden shackles
of luxury and lust
I was the first rebel
On your earth."

She considers her writings the outcome of protest.

She pours herself out both in poetry and fiction. Her famous anthologies are *Sahaj Sundari* (1965) and *Saptadas Asvarohi* (1974). She has authored over twenty novels, the prominent being *Sona Rupar Kathi* (1956),

Pap Punya Periye (1964), *Char Jan Ragi Yuvati* (1973) and *Paurush* (1984).

I met her at the Calcutta centre of the All India Radio where she was the Producer of spoken words. Our conversation turned to her creative writings. My first query was about her creative process, "There are some people who still subscribe to Mathew Arnold's point of view and believe that poetry is the spontaneous outburst of powerful feelings and that the poet does nothing more than just recording it. How would you react to this view? Please narrate your own experience of creating any one of your poems, say *Iswar Ke Prati Eve* (Eve to God), or any other poem you may like to take up."

She was frank, "I totally agree with Arnold's opinion. I would add a little bit that you may think of the moment when the first poetry in our history was born. Valmiki saw two love birds and when one bird was killed, suddenly something came out of his throat which is not 'gadya', which is not prose, which is something else. These are ordinary words but arranged in a way which made it a poetry, which is very powerful."

I quipped, "Valmiki's words sound like '*shap*', a curse". She continued, "Yes, but it is also a protest. Since love was killed, it is a protest against that. It was not a slogan that leftist writers raise, e.g. let us hold our flag high. Poetry is not slogan. It is different. It is something high, something elevated. I think the most of our poetry is in a form that is a protest—protest against the abnormal system, protest against abnormal situation, protest against crudity, protest against anti-love, protest against hatred and so on.

"You have referred to a very significant poem of mine. One poet once told me, 'If you die right now, Bengali literature would not lose anything because your poem *Eve to God* is there'. I have read Bible so many times right from my childhood. But when I saw the American film 'The Bible', suddenly a revelation came to me that Eve is the first rebel and not Adam. What type of rebel she is! She never liked that synthetic life where there is no pain, where there is no sin, where there is no cry, where there is no sorrow, no sadness. I think that without pain, without sorrow, without sadness, life is not complete. Chaos makes life complete. So I find that Adam is a very faithful son of God, but Eve is not, because Eve thought that life is incomplete without all these things and she must get knowledge. So she first touched the tree of knowledge, she first ate the apple. And she knew that there is a heaven and hell difference between nudity and dressing up. She came to know that after nine months labour and the consequent pain, she got something. She saw God's face in her child's face. So when I saw Eve touching the fruit in that film, immediately it came to my mind that 'Oh there is another meaning, another expression.' As you know, the central theme of my writings is that women get tortured. I think women are better souls. Women are better equipped. Such incidents prove that Eve is more sensible than Adam".

I commented, "Now coming to protest, it appears that protest of the present day Eve is, to a great extent, at the conscious and intellectual level only. Wherever the protest is spontaneous and genuine, it is understandable. But it comes mostly from those Eves who are already rolling in comforts, but want more. Those who are oppressed and exploited day and night, generally do not protest, as if they have accepted their lot. At times, protest of the modern Eve sounds like a fashion. By all this, I mean that we have to distinguish between the genuine protest and the pseudo protest."

She affirmed, "Yes, there is a lot of difference between the genuine and the pseudo protest. During the Naxal period, I attended a seminar at Poona. Some non-Bengali writers asked me, 'What have you written on the Naxalites? We don't find any Naxal theme in your literature'. Even about the great Bengal famine only two-three writers wrote on that famine. Actually there are two types of protests, the pseudo-protest and the real protest. Why our writers make such protests which are pseudo protests and which you say, are at the conscious level only, because they want to show that they are abreast with all the modern happenings and trends. But basically they have no touch with the realities of life.

"Then, there is another type of protest which is very difficult of distinguish. Once a Manipuri writer told me that your Shankar writes very well, he writes on all the evils of the society. This is not true, but I cannot prove it. Here the difference between the pseudo and the genuine protest is so fine that I cannot prove that Shankar's protest is a pseudo-protest, whereas Samaresh Basu's protest is the real protest. These pseudo-protests end up very soon. But when the protest is genuine and finds expression in the form of literature, it makes an ever-lasting impact. For example, Rabindra Nath Tagore wrote many songs on the division of Bengal which took place in 1905. But since the protest was genuine and emerged from a very deep level, the songs are relevant even now. Thus, if the protest goes deep into the mind, it will leave an eternal impression. As a critic, I can immediately find out which one is the real protest and which one the pseudo protest".

I probed further, "Would you like to elaborate on this point with reference to some characters of your short stories or novels? Despite the right of freedom and equality enjoyed by the present Eve, her exploitation, we find, has not ended. The female exploitation has only changed its forms which have been sophisticated to such an extent that she herself happily falls into the male traps without realising that she is being entrapped, as these traps appear to satisfy her ego".

She said, "I have written a small article in Bengali *Āmāder Ghar Chayi* (We want a House). It was influenced, I am not ashamed to say, by Virginia Wolfes *A Room of One's Own*. Actually our women are innocent people. They think they are mothers, they are wives, they are sisters and all. They never knew that they are being used by others. Their mother-image, their wife-image and their sister-image are in fact nothing, when a woman crosses twenty. She finds that she is an object of lust and that she is being used. She realises that her used portions are worn out, her beauty has faded, her energy lost and that she cannot satisfy everybody any more and that everybody is angry with her as every body has his own expectations from her. The other thing is that women are so degenerated that they don't realise that they are being exploited. You know that even highly qualified women do not get suitable place. But they want quick money and all the comforts that money can buy. I always discard this trend and protest".

Most of my writings are of protest. There is one character in a short story of mine entitled *Chalte, Chalte*. During a long married life she felt that nothing was left. Her life had become mechanical. She will go to office daily in the morning, come back in the evening. She was so worn out that she did not know what to do. One day her younger brother brought a child. She loved that child, Instead, she had two or three abortions before as her husband said that he could not afford a child. Consequently she lost the capacity of bearing a child. Though she was keen to get that child, her husband would not permit. She was so much disgusted that she decided to end her life by swallowing some pills. But it was difficult to get so many pills from a single shop. So she thought of collecting them from many shops of her acquaintances and with this purpose she went to the area where she had lived with her parents and grew up. She succeeded in getting them there. During her search for pills, a boy recognised her and told her that during his childhood she was his ideal and he liked her very much. This brought a turning point in her thinking and she remembered many pleasant experiences of her life before marriage. Soon she felt that life was still worth living. She returned to her house in the evening and the depression overcame her. She thought of carrying out her decision. She put all the pills in a glass of water and when they were dissolved, she picked up the glass to drink it. But before it could touch her lips, her pet cat suddenly jumped over her, throwing the glass on the floor. Though this is not a story of direct protest, yet it is a protest in a way".

I observed, "Although, the story ended with the cat throwing away the glass, desisting her from carrying out her decision to end her life, this woman had already been transformed after visiting her childhood environment, particularly the boy who had recognised her."

She explained, "But it was not a calculated move to end the story like that, the ending came up almost spontaneously without any conscious effort on my part".

I asked, "Does it mean that you don't control your characters from beginning to end and that once you have created them they go out of your hands and grow in their own way?"

She said, "There is a magazine in which many writers of my time have given interviews. One writer has said, 'I first pick up the theme and then I develop the story'. But I don't believe in this. I make no such calculations for my stories. They are sort of outbursts."

I inquired, "do you subscribe to this belief of some writers that during the creative moments the author is possessed by some power and writes under that spell without working out anything at the conscious level?

She confirmed, "Yes, it is correct. You may believe it or not. When I write a story, I don't know what shape it will take. During the process of writing, it works like photography. My characters and their situations spring up in my imagination like a photograph with clear details as if I am seeing them with my own eyes. They are a reality for me at that time".

I remarked, "It means that you don't work too much on your writings consciously. They are the outcome of your intuition".

She replied, "Yes, intuition is the right word in my case. I go completely by intuition".

I observed, "The end of your stories and the culmination of your characters must be a surprise for you also many a time".

She confirmed, "That is true, They spring a surprise for me also".

Giving a turn to the conversation, I said, "Women psychology is portrayed by both male and female writers.

But some people think that male writers are not able to do justice to their female characters as they depict them from the male point of view. Do you think, there is any substance in this contention?"

Reacting strongly, she said, "No, I don't think so. A good writer is neither male nor female, he is a hermaphrodite. I don't think that if Sarat Chandra is to write on the labour pains of a woman, he will write less efficiently than I can. Just the opposite question arose when I wrote about prostitutes, about the women in the red light area. My husband asked me, 'How could you depict them? You have never gone to that area?' A similar question can be asked when an author portrays a syphillitic patient, has he to be syphillitic himself before he depicts such a character. If I am a good writer, I know all these things intrinsically. All I may need is a few more details about the character I am portraying. So I don't believe in such wild statements that a male writer cannot depict female characters and a female writer cannot depict male characters".

I added, "Another possible explanation of this phenomenon may be that at the time of creation the author transcends all the individual barriers and is in communion with the universal mind, which has no sex, caste or creed, and at that time the entire knowledge possessed by the universal mind becomes available to him".

She was reminded of a short story by Tagore, "Yes, definitely. This reminds me of a very significant story by Rabindranath Tagore "Stri-patra" which was also filmed. He depicted the central character Mrinal very minutely. She tells her husband that the difference between your drawing room and our inner room is like the two sides of a woollen sweater—the outside it is all smooth and bright, but inside there are lots of loops, knots and ugly spots. How could Rabindranath depict Mrinal so minutely? He would not have knitted any sweater, I think. So a good writer is always a hermaphrodite".

Now, I touched upon another issue, "Many characters of your novels and short stories must have been drawn from life itself. Did you every find that your assessment of them in the real life underwent a considerable change in the creative process and you felt nearer the truth? Could you elaborate on this with reference to any one of your characters?"

She replied, "Yes, it does happen. There were many people, who were defeated in real life. But when I took them in my stories, I never let them feel defeated. I remember a story of mine about a person who used to collect extras. During this period I completed this story and two novels. All my stories and novels cover incidents which occurred in the recent times. There was a boy who was kidnapped and later brutally murdered. All the murderers were arrested. There was another famous case of murder in Europe that of Idris. There are many such cases of social evils going on in our courts recently. All these form the subject of my short stories. In fact, there is no dearth of subjects, if we look around ourselves. Then, why restrict ourselves to sex and violence. There is a long arena of subjects to choose form".

I pursued further, "Do you avoid sex and violence in your writings consciously?" She was categorical, "No, never, I use it only when I must. But I don't exceed the limit. Another short-story of mine is about a shoe-shine boy who sits and works in front of a restaurant. He was murdered by some criminals of the area. When the police came and enquired from the manager of the restaurant, he showed complete ignorance of the incident."

I referred to something new 1 came across, "There is a new phenomenon that I came to know about here in Calcutta only. It is peculiar to us in Delhi that there is a flood of 'Pooja Anks' in the market for which authors are commissioned earlier and that authors earn considerable sum during the Pooja season by writing profusely on demand. I wonder how writers manage to maintain the quality of their writings when they are under pressure to write on demand. How do you manage to strike a balance between the quality and the quantity of your writings under such circumstances?"

She didn't appear happy with this tradition, "I can show you many 'Pooja Anks' which are with me. I started reading them, but could not go ahead. So I stopped reading them, because the writings published under the label of short stories are not short stories at all. Sometime back, a very eminent female Bengali writer whom you also know but I will not mention her name, came to our AIR studies. She asked me as to what I was writing those days. I told her that I had written two novels. She enquired about the paper for which I was writing. I told her that I did not write them for any paper as I write for no paper. She was surprised and remarked, 'How could you write if you are not writing for any paper?'

"Once Narendra Chakravarty, Editor of one of the most popular children magazine *Anand* asked me to write a novel for his magazine. Any other writer in my place would have written for him the novel in a couple of months, but I took two long years to complete it as I was not fully satisfied with it and kept on revising it. Finally when I was satisfied, I went to his office and told him that I had finished the novel. So I don't indulge in the vicious demand and supply cycle. I have a job and am not obliged to rush on demand."

I asked, "How many novels have you written?" She replied, "Twenty are in book form. But actually I have written about one hundred novels which have been published in various magazines. For publishing them in the book-form, you have to develop them but I have no time for doing that. Still I am working on one or two novels".

Then, I came to a delicate question, "Which out of these gratified you the most? Could you name some of them which satisfied you completely?"

She was spontaneous, "Yes, I can name three such novels. One is *Pap Punya Perye* (Beyond Sin and Virtue). It is the tale of one day only of a husband and wife as to how they find through the days offering that they really love each other. Though they are hurt by all the darts and arrows of the world, yet they are truly in love with each other. Like a statue they have weathered all the storms, thunder bolts and rains for many long years and though smeared and hardened from outside, inside they are intact and still soft and warm to each other. There is another novel *Pataner Viruddhe* (Against Fall) which is about the modern youth, how they behave and how they view life around them, how they go to villages and do social work amongst Santhals.

"The third one is an epic novel, running into three hundred fifty pages. Its name is *Paurush* (Virility). It was published only last month. In this novel, I have put three characters in contrast with one another. One is man and the other is woman. They are terribly afraid of life. Though the man is man and the woman is woman, yet they always behave like eunuchs. Against them I have pitched a eunuch who is the head of a Eunuch Society and who tries hard to establish himself or herself as a full man or woman and by watching that third character, virility of the other two male and female characters returns and they join the society as healthy persons. Through this theme, I have also depicted the eunuch society for which I had to do a lot of research work. This is a new thing for the Bengali literature. We don't know that these eunuchs have lot of fads about sexual mal-practices. It is really moving that the eunuchs who cannot produce a child come to our homes for singing and rejoicing on the occasion of marriages and births just for a livelihood. Is our Society not cruel to them, besides the cruelty of the nature they are enduring?"

Summing up the conversation, I asked, "A writer of your kind who has no inhibitions of any kind must have run into controversy many a time and subjected to motivated criticism. How do you react to such provocations?"

She was firm, "When any editor raises a finger at my writing, I ask him to either publish it as it is or return it to me straightaway. I will not allow anybody to fiddle with my manuscript. In so far as the motivated criticism after publication is concerned, I just ignore it. Reaction of the contemporary writers is generally not very good, but in my case they avoid eloquence because they will not be able to stand by it.

"Fortunately, most of my books have got fairly good reviews and there has been no untoward criticism. Anti-criticism has also some value. In a recent review of my short story Dr. Sharat Chandra Upadhyaya, one of our best critics, gave more space to my story as compared to the story of Santosh Ghosh, who is one of our top writers. Though he commented on Santosh's story, he had all the good words for my story. So adverse criticism I hardly get. But some critics say that I am an angry young woman, I am very much angry and at times anger mars my writings. Well, this is what they say. But I don't think that I write in anger. I don't think, I am that angry."

(Calcutta—29.9.1984)

*

Nirmalprabha Bordoloi

B. 20.6.1933, Sibsagar, Assam; *mt.* Assamese, *edn.* M.A., Ph.D., Dip. in Ling.; *car.* Teaching, Retd. Nehru Prof., Assamese Deptt., Gauhati Uni.; *Awards & hons.* Assam Sahitya Sabha Award, Sahitya Akademi Award*; President's Award on Children Lit.; *Ed.* 'Natun Assamiya' daily and 'Ramdhenu' monthly; *Pubs.* (in Assamese) *poetry* Bam Phiringar Rang, 1972, Dinar Pasot Din, 1977, Samīpesu, 1977, Antarang, 1978, Assamiyā Omala Geet, 1978, Sudeergh Din Aru Ritu*; author of about 1500 lyrics, many of them very popular; wrote songs for films, recorded for discs; *juv. novel* Chil Chil Chila, 1959, *essays* Assamar Loke Samskriti, 2 Vols., 1972, Sāhitya O Samskriti, 1987, *research work* Debī, 1995.

Of Sensibility and Fulfilment

A powerful imagist poet of the modern Assamese literature Nirmalprabha Bordoloi conveys through very few but carefully chosen words deep emotional impressions of our time. Her idiom is highly suggestive and her imagery is symbolical. Her range of feelings is vast, her mastery of form is astonishing and her attitude to life is constructive. Hers is the voice of the modern Indian woman, emerging boldly from the dark caverns of prejudice and injustice and searching her identity:

Where is my identity?
Is it in my garments?
Is it in my ornaments?
Is it in the language of my region?
No, I say no,
In my full-throated voice,
Oozing out of
Independent experiences,
Which I should transform
With unified sensibilities.

Though her poetry has resulted from her deep roots in the Assamese folk life, it is acutely sensitive to the problems of the present age. She depicts beautifully the rootlessness of the modern man:

In the smell of the
Autumn field
My father comes back to me.
In the smell of the new '*gamocha*'
I unfold fresh
From the shop
I find my mother again.
Where shall I leave myself

For my child
O, where indeed?

She laments the speed with which one gets alienated from oneself:

I have not met me for a long time
The distance only increases,
Mile after mile, a thousand miles.
I feel as it were
I am
After layer
On layer
On layer
In a dark fiery womb ...

Author of sixty-four books and about five hundred lyrics, her output is phenomenal. Her creativity is multifaceted. Besides being a popular lyricist, she has produced drama, opera, children literature and literary criticism. She was the Jawaharlal Nehru Professor of Assamese at the Gauhati University. Many awards and honours have come her way. A volume of her poems *Dinar Pasot Din* bagged her the Assam Sahitya Sabha Award. *Sudirgha Din Aru Ritu*, another collection of her poems, won the Sahitya Akademi Award. *Chil Chil Chila*, a collection of her writings for children got the Rashtrapati Award. Her minutely researched study on the *Sakta* cult has received many accolades.

I interviewed her early this year when she was in Delhi to attend the annual meeting of the Sahitya Akademi Executive Board.

Some people believe that poetry is not created, it just gushes forth like a fountain from within and the poet only observes and records. I wanted to know if Nirmalprabha also subscribed to this contention. I also requested her to recount her experiences during the creation of such lyrical poems as *My Mother*.

She said, "A poet's creations come from that area of the mind which is not all consciousness. For that reason one cannot say that a poet creates with a 'conscious' mind. But something works in the depths of his or her mind and that force belongs to him and that leads him to become a creator. In that sense we can say that poetry is "created." She was sure that her lyrical poems such as *My Mother* resulted from such a process, "The mind had been storing up—both consciously and unconsciously—various experiences of my life and their related images. The poems, she feels ultimately come out from such sources when the creative impulse started working over them from time to time."

I wanted to know if she differentiates poetry from a poem, "Poetry is highly elusive, a poem is comparatively easy to write. Poetry flows from the subconscious, whereas the language in which it is recorded in the form of a poem is a product of the conscious. Hence, a gap between the two. But the impact of the poetic flow on the language makes the latter highly suggestive to enable the reader or listener to grasp it subjectively."

Nirmalprabha Bordoloi said, "To be a living thing a poem must be electrified with the spirit of poetry—That is how she would like to think of the relation between 'poetry' and 'a poem'. Not all poems contain poetry in the same intensity or depth. *Poetry* is like a spirit and a *poem* is an embodiment of that spirit."

Bordoloi's poetry reveals her intense love for nature. I was obviously keen to know what attracts her in nature more than the predicament of the modern mind. She explained that apart from the 'predicament of the modern man (or mind)' what has drawn her to the theme of Nature is its innate attraction. Nature is to her basically a mystery as well as the ultimate source of life. Both these feelings have been dominant in her.

Bordoloi has composed many a lyric meant to be sung and they have earned the admiration of listeners. Composing a song demands conscious effort from the poet. I asked her if that comes in the way of spontaneity. She was convinced, "All creations, to be charged with 'life', must ultimately come from a source deeper than the level of 'conscious efforts'; but conscious efforts too may be necessary for the final form that a poem or a song comes to take. Only when such 'conscious efforts' are not guided by the deeper spirit of the mind—the real creative spirit—artificiality or lack of spontaneity results."

Nirmalprabhaji is a popular poet and must have experienced the disadvantages of popularity. I wanted her to tell us how she managed to strike a balance between quality and quantity.

She explained, "There are more than one or two levels at which a poet or a creative writer may work. When he works at the deeper levels of his creative personality, he obviously works at a level that is not in tune with what may be called popular literature. On the other hand, there may be occasions when a writer may try to be available also at that level and on such occasions he may write songs or even poems which may be *popular* in the usual sense of the term. This is one way in which the problem of quality and quantity may be tackled in the field of literature. Only the serious readers are capable of responding to the creations that come from the deeper level."

I then asked her if her profession as a teacher ever hinders the natural development of her poet; as the poetic eruption knows no appointed time.

Nirmalprabha Bordoloi feels, "The teacher's profession may really become a problem for a creative writer if he does not learn how to protect himself—his deeper self—from the bad effects that profession may have. The artist may be lost in the teacher if the artist or the poet does not remain silently or secretly alert within him about that possibility or danger. If that basic problem is tackled in the right way, one can also tackle the related problem of what is called 'poetic eruptions'. Otherwise 'poetic eruptions' may create problems."

Nirmalprabha has won many literary awards. Does she think that they encourage genuine writing or just end up in fostering non-literary competition? I wanted to know how she views them as a writer. She told me, "The institution of *awards* may be both defended and argued against. Awards, when given on the basis of real literary assessments, can contribute something positive to the literary culture or atmosphere of a society. On the other hand, in the absence of proper alertness on the part of the practitioners, awards may also create problems."

To conclude, I asked her what her idea of a poet's fulfilment was. Nirmalprabha Bordoloi was very clear that a poet may experience a sense of 'fulfilment' when his or her silent preparations are seen at some stage to result in some satisfying creations. She herself had this type of experience on several occasions in her life. She also mentioned some of her poems in this context. She added that we may also experience a sense of fulfilment when we find one or two persons whose sensitivity has properly responded to our inner realisations. She has also had this sense of fulfilment.

(New Delhi—25.3.1994)

*

Vijaya Rajadhyaksh

B. 5.8.1933, Miraj, Maharashtra; *mt.* Marathi; *Edn.* M.A., Ph.D.; *car.* teaching, retired Prof.-Head, Marathi Deptt., S.N.D.T. Uni., Bombay, now Prof. Emeritus in this Uni.; *Awards & hons.* Best Short Story Collection Annual Award, Maharashtra Govt.—thrice, A.R.S. Jog Best Book of Criticism Award, Keshavrao Kothavle Best Book Award, 1991, Sahitya Akademi Award, 1993; *Pubs.* (all in Marathi) *short story collections* Adhantar, 1965, Timba, 1965, Videhi, 1972, Anolakhi, 1973, Akalpit, 1976, Parambyā, 1976, Ughadmeet, 1978, Kaman, 1978, Chaitanyāche Oon, 1981, Pangāra, 1983, Hunkār, 1984, Donāch Rang, 1985, Akherche Parv, 1988, Anāmikā, 1990, Vijaya Rājadhyakshānche Nivadak Kathā (selected short stories), 1990, *essays* Kadamb, 1979, Avatibhavati, 1982, Swacchand, 1987, *crit.* Kavitārati, 1981, Jihvār Swanandache, 1981, Samvād (Interviews), 1985, Ādimayā, 1990, Mardhekarānchi Kavitā, 2 Vols., 1991.

The Changing Human Perspective

Viaya Rajadhyaksh occupies a prominent place among the leading writers in Marathi. She started her literary career thirty-five years ago as a short-story writer and she has remained loyal to this form all these years. She has fifteen collections of short stories to her credit. Later she diversified to literary criticism, in the course of her doctoral research work, on B.S. Mardhekar as a poet, and has since published five volumes of critical studies.

The characters in her short stories are drawn mainly from the urban middle class, to which she herself happens to belong, and have within that limit a wide variety. They reflect in a suggestive manner the change that has been coming over the ethos of that class. The main concern of her stories is human relationship and her women characters are by and large nearer the centre of the stage than men. The transformation in the life of women after the World War II has been more pronounced than in the life of the male and her stories concentrate on this aspect. The narrative element in her fiction is minimal, the emphasis being on psychological probing, but she steers clear of the acrobatics of psycho-analysis. Several of her short stories have been translated into quite a few other Indian languages, and some into English. And they all have been very well received.

She retired from her long teaching career recently and is at present Professor Emeritus in S.N.D.T. University. She considers her long experience as a teacher rewarding and fulfilling as, according to her, her contact with young people, close in the case of a large number, has provided her with an empathy for the young that enriched her as a writer. She has won many awards and distinctions, including the noted Keshavrao Kothavle Award and the Sahitya Akademi Award.

I met her at Bombay last year during my lecture-tour to three universities on our western coast and had a full-length discussion with her on her creative writing.

In her opening remarks Vijaya Rajadhyaksh observed. "I have been writing short stories for the last thirty-five years, and have published so far fifteen collections. My earlier short stories were mostly romantic. This being a natural phase, I made no attempt to curb it. I think, any conscious effort on the part of a creative writer to check or change the trend of his writing is bound to end up in affected writing. My further collection, *Adhantar* (In the Air) with stories like *Bhaas* (Illusion) and *Tada* (Crack) represents this phase."

I wondered why she made no mention of her novels and inquired, "You must have written novels too. Could you name some you consider your best?"

She admitted frankly, "No, I have not tried my hand at this genre. Many people have been suggesting that I should now turn to writing novels. I also sometimes feel like doing so. But this is not enough. There must also be an inner urge. Not just pressure from well-meaning readers. And yet, the feeling that I should attempt novel-writing has been gathering strength. Maybe, I shall get down to writing it before long."

I probed further, "Like your readers. I very much hope that you do. However, are you fully satisfied with the short story as a medium providing satisfactory expression to all that is fluttering to come out from within? Would you name some of your short stories which have gratified you the most?"

She was modest in her reply, "I believe my best is yet to come. All sensible writers have this feeling, I suppose. Yet I can name some of my short stories which, I feel, provided me full satisfaction, or a sense of fulfilment, as a writer, because they turned out as I had conceived them. I consider *Akherche Parva* (The Last Chapter). *Deha Mrityuche Bhatuke* (The Body is a Toy in the Hands of Death). *Kamal* (Lotus), *Videhi* (Bodyless), *Purush* (Man), to name a few, as my best so far."

Coming to her creative process, I inquired, "You must have picked up many of your characters from real life. Don't you think you get to know them in almost absolute reality only during the creative act? Don't they then slip out of your hands soon and develop as they would, independently?"

She confirmed my contention, "Yes, I agree. Characters reveal themselves fully in the very process of writing, in a large number of cases; and they give the writer himself many a surprise. There is no conscious effort on my part during the creative act to control my characters. I just create them and try to infuse life into them. Then I leave them to themselves, yet following them quietly. So often they take a sudden turn which I had not thought of, and reveal unexpected peculiarities. There is my short story, *Anpadh* (Illiterate), for instance. The residents of a students' hostel are on strike, a turbulent one—a situation largely based on personal knowledge. The strike was directed against the rector, an upright man who always looked to the well-being of the students without any consideration for his comfort and convenience. His life became miserable, with the students becoming more and more rowdy. Finally at a meeting with them he settled the matter amicably. He shared his happiness with his wife, saying that they would live peacefully thereafter. But the wife, who had looked so meek and passive throughout the crisis, suddenly firmed up with her native strength lying dormant till then, said to her husband, 'This house that has caused us such undeserved suffering is not worth living in any more. Now that the trouble is over, we must leave it—and that too immediately.' When I started on the story I had never imagined that the frail woman was capable of such strength and wisdom. She gave a surprise, a pleasant surprise, to me too."

I observed, "Wisdom does not come automatically from formal education, not even from higher education. It depends on many other factors, such as the *sanskaras* imbibed from the parents, the family and the social surroundings, etc. The present system of education produces only literates, and not educated people in the proper sense of the term. I came across a very true definition of education in the form of a saying, 'Education is the ability to meet life's situations'. That way, I feel, our illiterate mothers were far more learned than the present 'educated' women, as they could face any situation in life unperturbed."

She seemed to agree with my view and said, "This reminds me of my story *Akherache Parva* (The Last Chapter). There is the husband running after women. He had three affairs. And then he leaves his wife to fend for herself and her children. But the woman, who had had little education, worked hard in order to rear her children properly. In a few years the family achieved a little prosperity. Then the husband showed up—old and shattered. He wanted to stay elsewhere, but his wife offered him a room to himself. A formal and correct relationship was established between them. The repentant husband asked her how she could achieve all this. She spoke of her struggle, and of how the instinct for self-preservation, conquering the one for self-destruction, had given her the strength to keep her home intact. That the near-illiterate women would rise to such a height and achieve maturity was a surprise to me too. Another pleasant surprise as the story goes on unfolding itself: a character developing on its own, leaving its creator astounded to watch it."

I raised another point, to elicit her views on the modern women. "The modern women wants to live an independent life. She would not like to depend on anybody, not even her husband. Don't you think it is a reaction to centuries of crippling dependence on man?"

She continued, "Yes, I agree. Man is a social animal. Man or women can live alone only for a short spell, but not for ever. One of my stories, *Jhoka* (Cradle) is on this theme. A career woman decides to live an independent life—all alone, despite the fact that her relations with her husband are cordial. She was transferred to another place, and her experiment of living alone profited by it. After some time an old destitute female relative of hers came to visit her. And feeling that she must give the woman the support she needed, she persuaded her, in all earnestness, to continue to stay with her, for good."

Delving into her creative act, I asked, "Some writers say that during the process of writing some power from within takes possession of them and they write under its spell. Do you share this experience?"

She thought for a while and observed, "This does not happen always. Some of my short stories, I must say, were written under such a spell. For example, *Andharacha Artha* (The Meaning of Darkness) and *Morpees* (Peacock Feather), to mention just two. On the completion of each of them I myself wondered if I had written it. This is a strange experience, very difficult to explain. You can neither invoke, nor shun, such a state. You are suddenly taken over by some mysterious power, and you write as if you were its instrument."

Coming to the role of the gender in creative writing, I inquired, "Some women writers have been feeling of late that male writers are not able to do full justice to their female characters— something that female writers alone can do. Do you find any substance in this view?"

She was emphatic in her reply, "I don't agree with this contention, in general. Great writers of the past, as also of our own times, have portrayed their female characters with great skill and profound understanding. But there are certain areas of life of which woman has more intimate experience than a man can possibly have. Child-birth is one such experience. In one of my stories, *Videhi* (Bodyless) the husband insists on being with his wife throughout her labour-pains. It was altogether a new experience for the husband who thus realized the sufferings of the mother in giving birth to her child. As a result, not only his love for his wife, but his respect for womanhood, increased greatly. For him too, a co-sufferer as it were, it proved to be an experience of creation."

Touching upon another controversial issue—literary criticism, I inquired, "You must have borne the brunt of the onslaught of your critics. How did you react to that? Would you like to comment on the relevance of the present day criticism to creative writing?" She observed, "There is some criticism on my work as a short-story writer, but not much. Some of the reviews were adverse. But a writer can not afford to be oversensitive, or too thick-skinned, in this matter. He should only take serious cognizance of such criticism. Criticism is, of course, useful. But, to be frank, there is no tradition of worthwhile literary criticism in Marathi, However, hope is held out by certain new quarters where literary criticism seems to be taking shape."

Referring to her onerous work-load as a teacher coupled with the household responsibilities which women cannot afford to evade, I asked her if they created any problem for her as a writer. She replied, "I was in the academic profession for almost thirtyfive years, and I am still involved in it. The profession was not only no hindrance to my writing, it also enriched me as a writer. A teacher who knows his business exposes himself to the fresh, impressionable and inquisitive minds of the young students. There is an interaction between him and them. And they are from a variety of backgrounds. Rapport with them sharpens his understanding of human beings and deepens his insight into human relations. Together they explore the world to which books provide a passport. Teaching takes on a creative dimension in such a situation. Of course, it is not every teacher who gets students capable of such rewarding interaction, but I have been fortunate in this respect."

(Bombay—22.9.1994)

*

Padma Sachdev

B. 17.4.1940, Jammu; *mt.* Dogri; *car.* Staff Artist, A.I.R., now writing; *Awards & hons.* Sahitya Akademi Award*, 1971; *Pubs. Dogri Poetry* Meri Kavitā: Mere Geet*, 1969, Tawi Te Chanhā, 1976, Nheri Galiān, 1982, Potā Potā Ninbal, 1987, Uttar Vāhinī, 1992; *Hindi Poetry* Meri Kavita; Mere Geet (in trans.), Sabad Milāvā, *Interviews* Dīwānkhānā, Mitvāghar, *novels* Ab Nā Banegi Dehrī, Nausheen, *travelogue* Main Kahtī Hun Ānkhin Dekhī.

Poetry: A Gift from Above

Padma Sachdev is a popular modern poetess of Dogri. Her love for nature is phenomenal. When innocent and carefree nature awakens and stretches itself in her poetry, its splendour overwhelms her:

"Is this the scattered rice?
Scattered white pearls?
White colour splashed?
No, none, it is snow
Whatever the Creator wrote with the white feathered pen
It is that very letter."

In her poem "Chav" (Fondness) the image of wheat is superb:

"The wheat
As if the husband has laden his nymph
With gold from head to feet
Or on the arrival of Spring
Dyed her darling in yellow
Like her the wheat crop is radiant with joy
While passing I would have shaken it in a wink
I would have overwhelmed her
Had I been a draught of wind."

Imagery is the hallmark of her poetry. She is lost in ecstasy in the company of nature.

On my way back from a seminar in Goa I met her at Bombay and we discussed her poetry at length. My opening query was, "Some people believe that poetry is not created. It is rather a spontaneous outburst of powerful feelings. The poet only records it. Would you like to share your personal experience with us? You have not only composed poems but also popular lyrics."

Corroborating the contention, she replied, "It is true that poetry is not created. But it is also a fact that everybody does not experience poetry. Had it been so, anybody would have become a poet. I think, some gifted persons only experience poetry. I began experiencing it right from my childhood. So I realised at an early age that poetry is not created. It is a sort of enlightenment, a revelation. Something gets cooking up within you. When it is the right time for it to come out, some hidden power overcomes the poet and he or she writes under a spell. It appears to him that he neither stands on the earth nor does he fly in the air, but is suspended from somewhere inbetween. He undergoes an experience of splendid weightlessness. I am amused when people say that they are going inside with a pen and paper to create a poem. On the contrary, I can say that poetry comes to you on special occasions when you are all alone. If somebody is with you it will shy away."

To get an idea of her creative processes, I enquired, "Did it ever happen with you that you felt restlessness within, something swelling up inside, rather keen to come out and it appeared that the time for its emergence was approaching, but suddenly it stopped half-way and could not be captured despite your best efforts, leaving the poem incomplete?"

She emphasised the point again, "There is a set moment for the poem to materialise. If you don't capture it there and then, it just disappears. I say this from my personal experience. If you did not make use of the moment instantaneously, you would lose it for good. You may have a better thing later, a new thing altogether, but the one you have lost will never recur. It so happens with me that whenever I feel the urge to write, the thing gets completed at one go. But if it fails to get completed for any reason, more often than not, it is lost. My poems usually do not remain incomplete, because whenever I feel the urge, I lose no time in recording it. But sometimes it so happens that somebody calls at you during that time, a doorbell or a telephonic call, then that thing remains incomplete, never gets completed. I have experienced another phenomenon. If ever a left over incomplete poem gets completed, it turns out to be superb, though this happens rarely, one of my poems is entitled *Des-Nikālā*, When I shifted from Jammu and joined All India Radio at Delhi, one sentence haunted me all the time: *Kaun kehta hai ki mujhe des-nikala nahin mila?* (Who says that I have not been exiled). Despite being in your country, the attraction of your home town, where you were born and brought up is irresistible. So this sentence persisted on and on until it developed into such a beautiful poem that of all my poems which I recite in public this one comes out the best, profusely applauded by the audience. I also like it very much as I have experienced the pangs of the exile myself."

Her poetry is inspired by the exquisite beauty of nature. This prompted me to observe, "You have not only seen nature from close quarters, but have also identified yourself with it and it permeates your heart as well as your hopes and ambitions. The charming beauty of nature abounds in your poetry. But nature has appeared in your poetry more in the form of memory, and less as the experience of the present. Why would your poetry be found dumb when you were face to face with nature?"

She felt the pinch of the question and replied, "No, not at all. Many of the poems you read in Hindi translation were written there. But those in which I was reminded of my home town were written after I felt Jammu. The fact is that I was brought up with nature. In 1947 my father Prof. Jayadev Sharma died during the partition turmoil. He was a great scholar of Hindi and Sanskrit. My milk-teeth fell only after his death. I had two younger brothers, one very young and the other not so young. I was the eldest. There was none to whom I could look to for friendship. I had a feeling from a very tender age that I was different from others. The one who talked to me from within could not talk to everybody, the way the earth hugged me could hug none else. With this feeling I thought from the very childhood that I was a specially gifted person. I don't feel like that now. I have rather been disillusioned.

"I liked always that our house was at the hill-top. The name of my village is Purmandal where we stayed for a year and a half after the death of my father. This village is mentioned in the Vedas also. It has its own importance. Since it was on the hill, I often roamed about in the jungle. The sons of my uncle often feared that I would be taken away by a wolf, but none dared touch me. I knew about all the trees there and could tell how many leaves each one had as also when each of them would bloom. I also knew about all the nullahs and also which one was flooded in rains and when. I knew how high we should climb the hill to touch the sky. I had a rich experience of these things in my childhood."

Many of Padma's poems appear to be the outcome of her anguish, to mention a few—*Meri Asha* (My Hope), *Pichhle Varsh* (The Last Year), *Talab* (The Urge), *Merī Āwāz Dūb Gayī*" (My Voice Sank), "Des-Nikala" (The Exile). When I inquired about their background, she observed, "When I shifted to Delhi, I remained mute and motionless for many days. I forgot that I write poetry, because my roads, the hill and jungle of my home town, my rivers, where I liked to roam about freely and all alone, were left behind. I remembered them immensely and intensely. The first lyric I wrote after somewhat recovering from the shock was entitled *Merī Āwāz Dūb Gayī* (My Voice Sank), in the noise of this country, in the hurry to reach somewhere every lyric of mine drowned, my voice sank. Then I wrote *Des-Nikālā* also. I felt the pangs of leaving my home. I had my personal compulsions. Sardarji also belonged to Delhi. If I was to join him in future, it was necessary for me to come to Delhi. The situation in Jammu took such an ugly turn that I could not stay there. Had I been an ordinary girl like those foolish ones who feel happy in going to Delhi after marriage, I would have been pleased. But it was not so. Even now I feel piercing pain in my heart when I remember the fact that I was forced to leave my home town. This very anguish gets reflected in my poems again and again. Whenever I write a poem I may be anywhere physically, but mentally I feel I am in my village. This is why I did not find it difficult to locate myself as I had never separated myself from my town. I am still there, clinging to some branch of a tree. People think I am here, but I am not here in reality."

One of her poem is entitled *Manzil* (Destination)—

"Whenever I am all alone in my house
Or within the closed doors of the studio
A destination comes and stops near me
Signals me to come nearby
I have no idea of its location
Yet I am tempted to approach it
Whenever this temptation crosses the limit
I hold fast with fear my *Anchal*
Lest I lose even these camping sites in an
Effort to reach the destination."

I asked her to throw some light on the background of the sense of fear reflected in this and other similar poems.

She explained, "It so happens sometimes that your past comes near you, raising suspicions about your future. He whose past has been full of hurdles is always suspicious of his future. I don't think that I have reached my destination. It appears to me that I am still in the train. Whenever a station arrives, I get down, take a glass of water and some snacks and come back to my compartment. But I am sure, the train will stop somewhere which will be my destination, my home."

Padma Sachdev has also gone through the terrible disease of Tuberculosis. She came out of this wretched state with her strong will-power only. Pointing to those trying times, I observed "Many of your poems like *Doli* (Palanquin) seems to be the offshoot of pangs of separation, rather migration as also the long disease. You must have realised the role of poetry in such trying situations. Could you share with us the backdrop of this poem."

She replied, "I wrote this poem when I was in a hospital. I was there for three years down with T.B.

I wrote many poems during those days. Then I remembered Jammu very much. When the snow fell and the roads got blocked, it appeared as if I was thrown away in wilderness, cut off from the entire world. The feeling of separation overwhelmed me at that time. There are many such poems full of disappointment, all the product of hospitalisation."

She has also written songs for films. Referring to this new dimension of her poetry, I inquired, "Writing songs for films must be different from those written under the inner urge. Would you like to elucidate the difference, taking one of your lyrics composed for films?"

She quipped, "I was not enamoured of switching over to films. I knew that it was not a firm ground. I knew about many people who wrote for films. A film entitled *Prem Parbat* was produced by Ved Rahi. Its songs were composed by me. Rahiji is also from Jammu and a famous fiction writer in Dogri. I composed them on his persuasion. Jayadevji had provided the music. I didn't have any difficulty with him. He composed the tune, narrating the situation, and I composed the song there and then. One of the songs was

'Yah nir kahan pe barse hai,
Yah badri kahan se ayi hai?'

and the other was

'Mera chhota-sa ghar-bar
Mere angana mein'

"I also wrote songs for a film produced by Rajinder Singh Bedi. But this film could not be released as Bedi Sahib fell sick and later died. There were some shortcomings in the film, I was told, which his son wanted to remove, but even he could not release it and passed away.

"If those who take work from you are nice and accomplished, you enjoy the work. It was a matter of privilege to work with Bedi Sahib and also with Jayadevji who was devoted to music. I remember, when I told Dinakarji that I wrote songs for *Prem Parbat*, he retorted, 'Since when have you started sharing the left overs?' I felt odd and gave up the very idea of writing for films."

Winding up the discussion, I emphasised the role of translation in bringing closer the literatures of different languages and observed, "I understand, you translate your Dogri poems into Hindi yourself. This, no doubt, lends authenticity to the translation, but it involves some risk also. While rendering his or her poem into another language the poet is often tempted to improve upon the original which may result in disturbing its basic concept. Do you care to check this tendency while rendering your poems into Hindi?"

Explaining her modus operandi, she said, "I have found out a midway. It is very difficult to translate the poems that are in specific metres. I never compromise in their case. At most, I would change a word here and there to adjust it to the target language. But in the case of those in free verse, the equivalent words come out spontaneously. Whenever I go to a poetic symposium I decide there and then what to recite, keeping the audience and the occasion in view. I keep the original Dogri poem before me and render it into Hindi spontaneously. There are some poems which lose their efficacy in translation. I recite them as they are in Dogri."

(Bombay—3.1.1984)

*

Indira Goswami
(Mamoni Raisom Goswami)

B. 14.11.1942, Gauhati, *mt.* Assamese, *edn.* M.A., Ph.D., *Car.* Teaching, presently Professor in Assamese, Dept. of Modern Indian languages, University of Delhi, *Awards & hons.* *Sahitya Akademi Award—1983, Assam Sahitya Sabha Award—1988, U.P. Hindi Sansthan Sauhard Samman-1992, Katha Award for Literature-Delhi-1993, *pubs. Assamese*—short stories Chinaki Maram—1962, Kaina—1966, *Hridaya Ek Nadinam*—1990, *Tej Aru Dhulire Dhusrit Prishta*—1994; *novels Chenabar Srota*—1972, *Neelkanthi Braj*—1976, **Mamare Dhara Tarowal*—1980, Ahiron—1988, *Une Khowa Howda*—1988; *autobiography Adha Lekha Dastavez*—1988, *English* (in translation) *The Shadow of the Dark God*—1986, *Selected works of Indira Goswami*—1988, *An Unfinished Autobiography*—1990, *Saga of South Kamrup*—1993, *research work—Two Ramayanas from the Valleys of Ganges* and *Brahmputra*—1996; *Hindi* Neelkanthi Braj—1988, *Jivan Koi Sauda Nahin*—1992, *Indira Goswami Ki Kahaniyan*—1996, Short stories translated in other Indian languages also.

Imaginative Flights of Reality

Indira Goswami, Mamoni Raisom Goswami to her readers, has carved a niche for her among the prominent Assamese fictionists who, transcending their regional borders, have figured at the national level. She is known mainly for her concentration on the tragic plight of our women in a repressive world of suffocating socio-religious conventions set for them by the male-oriented system, though she uses a wider canvas in her writings to enrich them with many socio-cultural and economic issues concerning the lower and down-trodden strata. Her own life has been full of turmoil resulting in pain and agony brought about by the decadent social order and natural calamities. But it is heartening that her earlier sufferings have not ended up in bitterness, but have been transmuted into sympathy for the sufferers intensely reflected in her fiction.

Her short stories and novels represent an amalgam of real life experiences tempered with imaginative flights. She herself admits, "I have moulded these sometimes hard and painful and sometimes happy and exhilarating experiences with my imagination. To me imagination is like a pattern of petals in a flower bud. The flower can bloom only with the unfolding of these petals through stark practical dealings with life." Her famous novel *Mamare Dhara Tarowal* (The Rusted Sword) which won the Sahitya Akademi Award, brings out the plight of the labourers engaged in building an aqueduct over the Sai river in Rai Bareli district. *Chenabar Srota* (As the Chenab Flows) portrays the sufferings of the poor workers employed in the construction of a bridge on the basis of her personal experience at the construction site. Similarly, in her novel *Nilkanthi Braj*, translated in English as *The Shadow of a Dark God*, she narrates the pathetic life of widows and spinsters, their sorrows and agony, their desires and frustrations, as she witnessed them at Vrindavan. Her other famous novel *Une Khowa Howda* (The Tusker's Moth-eaten Saddle) paints an undiluted and vivid picture of awful environment polluted by religious superstitions and meaningless ritualistic activities, coupled with the untold atrocities perpetrated on young widows in the garb of religion. Her short stories also reveal the unending miseries woman have to go through in every walk of life.

In her autobiography *Adha Lekha Dastavez* (An Unfinished Autobiography), she writes about herself in disarming frankness, hiding almost nothing and unmasking everything with blatant charm and with the dictum 'I acted as I thought'.

I was drawn to her writings for their moving portrayal of the 'have nots'. We got an opportunity to sit and discuss various dimensions of her writings, the inner processes involved in their creation and other aspects of this arduous and breath-taking activity.

Opening the conversation I asked, "You have mentioned almost emphatically in your 'selected works' that you have drawn your main characters from real life. Drawing characters from real life has its own advantages as well as disadvantages. It does lend authenticity to the work, but at the same time tends to curb the imaginative flights so essential for a work of fiction. Could you recount any instance when you got stuck up mainly because the character from real life was so dominant that it arrested your imagination and posed a big problem in your creative process, particularly in your novels *Una Khowa Howda* and stories like *The Offspring*."

She thought for a moment and then opened out, "Yes, I have drawn some of my characters from real life. I have never felt any disadvantage for this. It never curbed my imagination because I have used only a fragment of the real character and the rest is moulded with my imagination. I never got struck up due to the real character being dominant or otherwise, because I borrowed only a particular aspect or quality of the real person and then used my imagination to create the fictional character. Thus, in my novel *Une Khowa Howda* most of the characters have been based on real life characters, but were moulded by me in the fictional form. In my story *Offspring* the heroine was known to me in real life. Some of the characters, like the sensitive adhikar of the sattre in *Une Khowa Hawda* and Udhya Bhanu, the alcoholic of my novel *Udhaya Bhanu Charitra* were very close to my heart. But the intimacy did not restrict the flow of my imagination. On the contrary, I could mould these characters with deeper feelings and intensity".

Then I took up her famous novel *Neelakanthi Braj* and enquired, "Your novel *Neelakanthi Braj* appears to be based on your intense personal experiences in your life. What was it that inspired you to transcend the personal pain and agony to give the Brajbhumi a vibrating personality of its own, so vital for any regional novel worth the name?"

She replied, "Yes, you are right, *Neelakanthi Braj* is based on the experiences of my own life at Vrindaban. This city itself has become a kind of character of the novel. I loved Vrindaban and was very inquisitive about its people, the pilgrims who came there and the temples, bye-lanes and lanes of this ancient and historical place. I read books about its history and the past turmoil and blood-shed caused by the Afghan invaders. I was shocked by the condition of widows, mostly Bengali women, left to die in this holy city and wrote about them in my novel. These women were mostly from East Pakistan (now Bangladesh) i.e. from Dinajpur, Rajsahi, Bhakura and other places. I saw undefinable poverty and inhuman condition of these widows. I myself was passing through a tragic period that time. My beloved husband Madhavan Rayasom was killed in an accident. He was only twenty-nine years old at that time.

"All this became a part of my own mental agony and it poured out of my pen almost spontaneously in the novel and formed a portrayal of Vrindaban, as seen and felt through my senses, during the period 1969 to 1970."

Indira Goswami was brought up right from her childhood in the bounties of the nature which shaped her. This prompted me to ask her, "You have enjoyed the beauty and bounty of nature by living amidst it, first in Assam and later in other parts of the country. What was its impact on you and your characters?"

Welcoming the question, she admitted, "Nature has played a very important role in my life. I cannot think of any life without nature. In my early childhood, it was the natural beauty of Shillong, with its pine trees, lakes, streams and brooks that haunted me. I felt a kind of life force, a mystical aura in the surroundings of nature, in my childhood and even later on when I grew up. During my stay at Gauhati, the mighty Brahmaputra, became source of inspiration to me. I used to feel that somehow, mysteriously, the souls of the persons who were dear to my heart and who were no more, had been gathered to the basin of the Brahmaputra. Very often I used to think that my beloved mother was sleeping there under a net made of drops of water from this massive river. Whenever I saw the different moods of the Brahmaputra, this mysterious feeling overwhelmed me. Moreover, in my early childhood before going to Shillong, I spent many years in the bossom of nature in my village Amranga in south Kamrup, with its dense forests, green paddy fields and Jagalia river flowing by its side. I was always out of the house, roaming about with the village children among the rice fields or along the thick forest and river. Nature plays a vital role in my novel *Une Khowa Howda* (The Moth-eaten Howda). It centres around a sattra, a Vaisnavite monastry, in the remote corner of North East in the district of Kamrup in Assam. The adhikaras or the heads of sattras enjoyed immense privileges holding vast tracts of land. The condition of the people, mostly opium eaters, during the threshold of the Independence have been portrayed in this novel. The harrowing life of the Brahmin widows has been portrayed in great details. The river Jagalia, the green Matia Pahar (Mountain) and the thick forests where we used to roam about, have been brought out in this novel as they were. Even in my short stories, I depicted nature in abundance.

"I don't know why I don't have any attachment for snowy peaks of mountains. I always used to compare them with the white cloth covering coffins. My deep attachment lies with the brooks and rivers, oceans, trees and forests. The sound of the ocean water, especially in the mid night, gives me a kind of undefinable feeling. The foaming waves dashing against rocks is one of my favourite scenes. It is really very difficult to define how nature has entangled itself with my psyche throughout my life".

Knowing that hers has been a life of suffering, I remarked, "Some people believe that life is a compromise; if you don't get what you like, learn to like what you get. Do you subscribe to this view? You have lived a life full of turmoil. What sustained you the most in life as well as in creative writings?"

Almost agreeing with the contention, she said "Yes, I do believe that life is a compromise and every human being has gone through this experience some time or the other. Even in my days of turmoil, it was only creative writing which sustained me. I used to forget the pain of many unpleasant incidents while writing. Writing became my companion. It was like a fusion between life and the written word. Both existed side by side".

Then I posed a personal question: "Who knows the plight of the Indian woman better that you do? Have you ever been the victim of discrimination and exploitation in life and in literature?"

She appeared to have some reservation in taking up the question at the personal level. Yet she replied, "I have never given any thought to the question, whether I have been victimised or discriminated against. But I have seen in general that Indian women writers have not been given due recognition in some of the important representative works on Indian literature. I have also seen exploitation of women to a great extent in my life. I have written about the terrible exploitation of the Brahmin widows in my novel *Une Khowa Howda*. I have seen and written about the exploitation of women labourers in private construction companies, economically as well as sexually. They were never given equal wages even though they worked harder than men. I have witnessed all this with my own eyes, when I stayed near their camps on the work sites while writing my novels like *Ahiran* at Korba (M.P.) and *Mamare Dhara Tarowal* at Rae Bareli (U.P.)".

Touching upon a controversial issue I asked, "Some people feel that only women writers can do justice to their female characters, male writers tend to either ignore or distort the feminine reality. Do you find any substance in this contention?"

Rejecting this view outright, she remarked, "No, I don't find any substance in this contention. There are superb pieces of writing by male writers who have portrayed female characters with unbelievable intensity and depth, which the women writers probably could not have done themselves. Who can forget *The Mother* of Gorky? or the *Whores of Kawabata* or *Lora* of Boris Pasternak in *Dr. Ziwago*? I would like to point out the character of Basant Kaur in the famous Punjabi novel of Sohan Singh Shital *Yuga Badal Gaya*. Even in Assamese literature, Homen Bargohain's female character in his novel *Subala* (1963) is a fascinating creation. The author has drawn the agony of the prostitute, Subala, with very realistic and poignant strokes of his pen. I doubt whether any women writer has ever portrayed a prostitute with so much intensity and insight in Assamese literature. In the context, I would also like to refer to Mirza Mohammad Ruswa (1858-1931) and his immortal portrayal of Umrao in his famous novel *Umrao Jaan Ada* (1899). It is based on the real life of a courtesan in Lucknow. Regarding his novel, Ruswa himself has commented, 'My novel should be regarded as a history of our times'. The character of Umrao is a fine example of a male writer, writing about a woman in clear, realistic and sympathetic narrative of great impact.

"I would also like to mention Ananthmurthy's *Samskara* and his heroine, a low caste woman. But it is not that women writers have lagged behind in writing deeply and intensely about women. We find a heart-rending portrayal of Phaniamma, a widow, in M.K. Indira's Kannada novel. The study of a widow's life from a female point of view, in such a realistic and mind-shattering way, is a landmark in Indian literature.

"Similarly, the agony and exploitation of women has been depicted by Amrita Pritam, Mahasweta Debi, Nirupama Bargohain and several other women writers. Unfortunately works by women writers writing in regional languages have not come to lime light due to lack of competent translation. Their proper assessment has not been made yet."

Her immense interest in the labour class led me to ask, "Were you ever involved in the labour movement that prompted you to take up the cause of the 'have nots' in your novels *Ahiran* and *Chinavar Srota*? If not, what was the other inspiration?"

Denying her interest in labour movements, she replied, "I have never been involved personally in any labour movement, but I have witnessed the life of labourers and other workers on construction sites of a private company. I had the opportunity to stay at the work site and observe with my own eyes the different activities of the workers and their problems.

"The reason for writing about the workers and the labourers, as you say 'have-nots', was their miserable plight, their exploitation and repression and mainly my innate sympathy with the down-trodden strata of our society. There still exists in Indian society considerable social and economical injustice among a certain section of the multitude. My object was to expose all this in my writings".

Coming to her autobiography, I observed, "Some writers feel that all creative writings are essentially autobiographical in one way or the other. If so, where lies the necessity of writing an autobiography exclusively, particularly when it is bound to be the secondary elaboration of the original happenings, guided by the inner psychic fortifications. Yet you indulged in writing

Adha Lekha Dastavez. What prompted you to write your autobiography?"

She reacted sharply, "It is only partly true that all creative writing is autobiographical. I may write in my novel about certain persons I know or certain events I experienced, but it is transferred to the pages in the novel, covered and camouflaged by my imagination, the inclination of my mood at the time of writing. So what comes out at the end is not an exact graphic account of that person or that event. But the autobiography is the sum total of what the writer has thought, or said or done, throughout his/her life. It is an expression of her inner, private thoughts and feelings. It is a factual representation of the events, the different persons (intimate or casual), the different places in the writer's life. There is hardly any place for imagination here.

"I have not written about the entire span of my life in my autobiography. It is an account of my life from childhood to the year 1970, i.e. about 30 years of my life. That's why it is called *An Unfinished Autobiography* in English and *Adha Lekha Dastavez* in Assamese.

"Actually it was the well known Assamese writer Homen Bargohain who prompted me to write about myself. His letter moved me and touched some inner cords in my heart, and I decided to write my autobiography. It began as a serial in a monthly magazine—But due to several reasons I stopped writing it after some chapters were published. After several years an editor of a publishing firm persuaded me to pick up the threads again, and complete the autobiography. So I resumed certain period in my life, i.e up to 1970. Here also I have covered only some incidents of my life".

Concluding the conversation, I asked "what is your concept of fulfilment as a writer? Many such occasions must have come your way. Would you like to share some with us?.

She was frank and fair, "I don't think complete fulfilment ever comes to a writer. He may feel happy due to a particular achievement. But complete fulfilment is probably not possible. Some good occasions have come in my writing career, but a kind of void has always remained in my heart.

"I feel happy with the colourful letters I get from my fans. I also feel extremely happy when I read in some of the letters that many of them get strength and solace after reading my autobiography.

"I was extremely happy when once I read in an Assamese magazine *Sutradhar* that one Raghvendra Deka, a Scientist, who was a member of one of the teams on expedition to the Antarctica, had left a copy of my novel, *Mamare Dhara Tarowal* (Rusted Sword), in their library in the icy waste land of the Antarctica, as a token of love from his wife, who is a fan of my writings—I also felt a strange kind of thrill and joy, when a fan from one of the villages in Assam told me that he used to carry one of my books and read it while ploughing his paddy fields.

"The immense love of my readers for my writings has given me more happiness and fulfilment than any award for my literary achievement.

"Out of all my books, my novel *Une Khowa Howda* has given me a feeling of fulfilment and satisfaction, to some extent."

(New Delhi—1.5.1996)

*

Pratibha Ray

B. 21.1.1944, v. Alabole, Distt. Cuttack; *mt.* Oriya, *edn.* M.A., Ph.D.; *car.* teaching and writing, presently Reader, Edn. Deptt., B.J.B. College Bhubaneswar; *Awards & hons.* Govt. of India, Edn. Deptt. Award-1977, Best Story Award of Orissa Govt.—1980, Orissa Sahitya Akademi Award—1985, Sarala Award—1990, Murtidevi Award—1991; *Pubs.* Oriya, *short story collections* Shreshta Galp—1984, Itivrittak—1987, Bhagwānar Desh—1991, Prithak Ishwār—1991, *novels* Punyatoyā—1979, Nīltrishna—1981, Shilāpadma—1983, Yajnasenī—1985, Uttar-Mārg—1988, Ādibhūmi—1995; *Hindi edns. (in trans.) short story collections* Devkī, Kālantar Katha; *novels* Draupadi, Konārk, Uttar-Mārg; prominent works translated in other Indian languages also.

Blending Reality with Spirituality

Pratibha Ray has a prominent place among the favourite fictionists of the modern Oriya literature. She has to her credit eighteen novels and ten short story collections. Her famous novel *Yajnasenī* delves deep into the inner recesses of the great Draupadi of Mahabharata and brings out her intrinsic strength to fight for her rightful place in the strife-torn society of prestige-stricken 'luminaries' who had lost their way in the wilderness of the complex value system of the age. Her other popular novels are—*Punyatoyā, Aranya, Nīlatrishnā, Silāpadma, Samudra-Svar, Aparichitā* and *Uttarmarg*.

She has made a mark as a short story writer also. Her prominent short story collections are—*Itivrittak, Abyakta, Asamāpta, Devakī* and *Kālantar-Kathā*. Her famous short story '*Bhadralok*' was telecast by Delhi Doordarshan in a serial. She is the recipient of two prestigious awards, Sarala Award and Murthidevi Award, besides many other awards. Many of her writings have been translated in Bengali, Telugu, Gujarati, Hindi and other Indian languages as also in English.

I had a chance to discuss with her at length the various dimensions of her creative writings during her recent visit to Delhi. My opening question was, "Many characters of your short stories and novels must have been drawn from real life. Could you recount any of them who got out of your hand and underwent a sea change in the creative process?"

This prompted her to reflect upon her creative processes and she opened up gradually, "It is not by chance that I am defined as what I am, within my culture. As a writer, I am connected to the world I live in through varied ties. I realise my talent and creative power in my culture and I draw necessary nourishment from my soil for the germination of my dreams. Hence, all the characters of my short stories and novels have been drawn from my culture. Yes, there are some real characters whom I have seen or heard and some do not exist in flesh and blood. They are, you may say, imaginary characters. But no imagination spurts out of imagination. Imagination is also culture-based. Creative ideas which are defined as spontaneous are not really so. The spontaneity is a psycho-cultural process. Therefore, some of my imaginary characters are not exactly that. In society, all my characters exist, of course, with different identities. Our subconscious and unconscious psyche are always active deep-rooted in our culture; when this surfaces in the conscious we refer to it as a spontaneous idea. Since nothing is completely imaginary and exactly spontaneous, my effort to give them form and understand their depth of experience transforms the characters into a total being. The society and myself might have viewed this total being only in a fragment. The characters whom I have visualised in an embryonic form in the long process of preparing myself to portray them, possess me. When I complete writing, I realise that truth has been revealed; that was inevitable.

"To give an example: You may recall the character *Sama Puhana* in my novel *Uttarmarga* (The Road After) which provides an account of the freedom-struggle in my own village area. I had heard one-line story about Sama Puhan that he was a vagabond, illiterate youth, the only child (son) of a farmer. He was inspired by seeing the procession of Satyagrahi's and moved by listening to the slogans like 'Bharat Mata Ki Jay', 'Mahatma Gandhi Ki Jay'. He untied the bullocks and without informing his parents joined the procession, giving slogans in a high pitched voice. He came to Cuttack. For some time holding a Tiranga flag, he was wandering from village to village spreading the message of Gandhiji to participate actively in the freedom struggle. He did not know who the Britishers were and what Freedom meant. But he was a dedicated voluntary freedom fighter. He never returned to the village again and what happened to him nobody knew and nobody bothered. His unfortunate parents waited optimistically that their son would return one day after Independence. They ultimately died after Independence. Whatever there was of Sama Puhan's property was grabbed by the relatives immediately. Now he is a forgotten name in my village area and in the history of freedom struggle, his role like many more Sama Puhans all over rural India is considered very insignificant. This is the factual evidence I gathered from the oldest person of my village who also never gave any importance to this rustic youth's role in the freedom struggle.

"But Sama Puhan is a very significant character in my novel. He could not have died a normal death. He would have sacrificed his life for the cause of the nation. Who knows what torture he would have undergone for his upright, obstinate determination to smash the Britishers heads with his bamboo stick? In my novel Sama Puhan was active till Independence and even after that. He joined *Bhoodan Andolan* responding to the call of Vinobaji. He mysteriously vanished after being beaten up by a land lord's gundas while he was on hunger strike in front of the land lord's place, begging extra land for the landless. You know, I have dedicated the novel to all the 'Sama Puhans of my country'. There are so many other characters, very insignificant in real life. But all have gone through a sea change in the novel, like Maithili and Sevati.

"I wrote their version only and I emotionally realised that no character is insignificant in his/her actual life. They are only neglected characters. Once you comprehend the depth of their experience, they emerge as most significant beings."

Curious to find out her aptitude for the form in fiction, I asked," You have written short stories as well as novels. Which one of these, you think, is your forte? Did it ever happen that you started writing in one form, say short story, and after working on it for some time realised that it had the potential of a novel and you switched over to that?"

She was a bit hesitant, "Excuse me, it is very difficult on the part of a writer to judge his/her own writing. My readers are the best judge to say which form, i.e. short story or novel, is my forte. Some of my critics say I am best suited for novels, some say the other way. If you ask me in which form I derive more satisfaction, I will say both. I have eighteen number of novels and seventeen short story collections. During the long journey, in the meandering path of the world of fiction, I have never started in one form say short story and after working on it for some time or even after completing it have reached the other form (novel). Of course, some readers have requested me to elaborate a short story into novel or to write a second part of a novel. But I could not have succeeded in fulfilling their request. My experience says that a short story cannot be expanded to a novel or a novel compressed into a short story. In both cases the art of both the forms will be lost. Moreover novel does not mean writing more pages and short story does not mean writing less.

"One may expand a short story into five hundred pages but only end up with a short story in an elaborate form. The element of novel may not be traced there. If at all one starts with a short story and ends with a successful novel, then it will be another story, not the same story being hidden in the subconscious at the time of first drafting. Of course, I wrote a short story on Sama Puhan, first titled *Some Day He will Return*. But my character Sama Puhan, though the same person in the novel, has undergone a sea change. And he is only one character in the novel among many more characters and the novel has probed into many socio-cultural problems of the time."

Now I turned to her famous novel *Uttarmarg* and asked, "In your preface to *Uttarmarg* you observed, 'This novel is not a history, it is a novel' and yet could not afford to ignore the history of the freedom struggle, rather made concerted efforts to lay your hand on the basic facts. How did you manage to strike a balance between fact and fiction in this novel?"

Picking up the thread, she replied, "As I have already written in the preface to the novel, history cannot afford to accommodate fiction; but a novel has to accommodate history in some form or other. How can a writer ignore history which is an integral part of the soil upon which his creative personality has evolved? Resting on history we live at present for the future. The experience of transient time has always been expressed in novels. An imprisoned nation's strugglings, hopes and sacrifices for ushering a better future, have been expressed.

"This has been brought about by filtering the historical facts, rejecting the inessential parts, adding some essential attributes to the characters and events which could have possibly happened at that time.

"Here the characters are made superior with intrinsic dignity and pride. The historical facts are potential seeds growing into majestic trees to sustain the burden of future. Sama Puhan may be an example of history being blended with the inner life of character and time; transcending history itself, not deviating from the ideology and philosophy of the character. The novel's structure is a synthesis of reality with imagination."

Then, I asked, be it *Yajnaseni*, *Silapadma* or *Uttarmarga* you have concentrated mainly on delineating the plight of the women who has suffered the most in our male-oriented society. What is it that prompted you to accord priority to the cause of the women? Do you believe that only women writers can do justice to their female characters?"

She was cautious in her reply, "I do not think you mean to brand me a feminist writer. Normally, if a male writer writes for the cause of men he is not branded as a male Chauvinist, but when a woman writes for the cause of women, she is branded as a feminist writer. Anyway, I would like to clarify that I am a humanist; and when I concentrate on women's problems, I concentrate on a social problem and write for the cause of human beings. Are not women human beings? Are not women's problems social problems? A writer is always prompted to give priority to burning problems of the society he lives in. When a problem—be it a problem concerning men, women, animals, environment—is accute, it leaves a deep impression in the sensitive mind of a writer and prompts him/her to give priority to that problem. Women's problems are much more in a male- oriented society, progressively made more accute and complex by the march of time.

"To answer the second part of your question, there is no definite answer. What I feel is the voice of a genuine artist is sexless and a true writer manages to cross the narrow boundaries of geography and gender while portraying a character. Oppression and exploitation of women in a male-dominated or patriarchal society has been the prime theme of the two great epics of the world, the *Ramayana* and the *Mahabharata.* This trend continued to be the central theme in Indian literature starting from Valmiki, Vyasa, Kalidas, Premchand, Sarat Chandra and many others. Even modern Indian male writers tend to depict oppression of Indian women with greater confidence and deeper involvement. Bankim Chandra Chatterji and Rabindranath Tagore had depicted women expressing rare courage and power in crucial moments of social oppression. Even Sarat Chandra Chatterjee, for his boldness in depicting strong women characters, was branded as a feminist by conviction.

"Here, of course, the writer's sex plays an important role in certain matters. Certain perceptions like mother's heart, pain and agony of child birth, the discrimination practised by women themselves in the upbringing of girls and boys from an early stage and oppression of daughter-in-law by the mother-in-law and *vice-versa* cannot be experienced and felt by men and thus when portrayed are likely to fall short of perfection. If *Ramayana* and *Mahabharat* would have been written by women writers, then Surpanakha's agony and inner feelings, Kakeyi's whole life's sufferings, Ahalya's sorrow, Sita's protest against injustice by Rama, Draupadi's traumatic experience of being stripped in front of royal court, would have been portrayed and protested more successfully. It is true that some parts of the women psyche remain opaque to man and *vice-versa*. The deep-rooted masculine thoughts and feminine thoughts tinged with cultural milieu may sometimes govern and textual and contextual aspects of literature."

Referring to the mythical element in her novel *Yajnaseni*, I asked, "The modern mind fails to grasp many a myth, such as 'Draupadi Chiraharana', 'Viswarupa', etc., hailed in our great epic *Mahabharata*, dismissing them as unbelievables in this age of science. Some modern writers, such as Bhyrappa in his Kannada novel *Parva* and Narendra Kohli in his Hindi novel *Mahasamara*, have attempted to reinterpret the past in the present context. But you do not appear to have attached much importance to reinterpreting the past for the benefit of the present. How would you react to this contention with reference to your novel *Yajnaseni*?"

Taking up the issue of myth in right earnestness, she observed, "In this post modern age of high technology and electronics, everything including humanity, super naturality, even mother's love has come under interrogation. Also, the modern mind lives in a complex political culture where derationalisation and dehumanization have been over-powering. My effort in *Yajnaseni* was to fight against the system which believes in the power of demon which spreads like fire, violence, hatred and inhumanity and disbelieves the super-natural power, dismissing myths as *Mithya*. Therefore, I did not endeavour to deviate the incidents of Draupadi's life and allowed the already spoonfed modern mind to give an insight into human life as Sanjaya in *Mahabharata* was giving insight to the blind Dhritarashtra. That the blending of spiritual authority with man's will power can save him from a great calamity has been symbolised by 'Draupadi's Vastraharan'. 'Viswarupa' symbolises the philosophy of the body as universe which gives great confidence and insight to the human mind. The Oriya Saints equated the body with the whole universe by '*Pinda* (body) *Brahmanda* (Universe) *Tattva*' delineated by *Pancha Sakha*. Understanding this philosophy, all distinctions of 'mine' and 'thine' are forgotten and realisation of supreme identity is achieved. Like the metaphorical use of languages in modern literature which conceals more than it reveals, these symbolic representations help humanization through self-realisation and realisation of Supreme identity.

"Reinterpreting the past for the benefit of the present for me is not attaching scientific reasons to incidents but inculcating human values through reinterpretation of the characters. My Draupadi has through-out pleaded for the welfare of mankind and raised her voice against moral decay and degeneration of personal honesty of Kauravas, Jayadratha, and ethical norms in social life. Even if experiencing great personal tragedy, suffering, exploitation, humiliation and various kinds of social decay, she has always pleaded for emotional integration, peace and harmony in the universe. She has taken bold steps against social evils like castism, trying to bring the underprivileged into the main stream. All these, in my opinion are reinterpretations of the past, keeping in view present state of the world. My Draupadi is a social reformer, begging for a nuclear-free civilization. At one stage in the novel she speaks that like Devi Sita she too could seek and find shelter inside mother earth, but that would be the undoing of the mission for which she came. She is revealed not to be the war-monger, but as one who rightly understood war to be a bloody and painful surgery needed to save the world."

Responding affirmatively to her concepts, I remarked, "You have rightly differentiated Draupadi from Sita. Draupadi shuns escapism and faces life and its complexities boldly. I do agree with your concepts of Draupadi's *Chiraharan* and Yashoda's glimpse of *Visvarupa* as annunciated by you in your reply, but where do we find them visualised in your novel?"

Reacting sharply to my query, she added, "Of course, it is very much there in my novel. To me, the episode of Draupadi's *Chiraharan* in the *Mahabharata* is meant to bring out, among other things, the basic truth that blending of spiritual force with will power can save man from even the greatest calamity and I have depicted it in my novel that way. Invoking the spiritual authority, Draupadi raised her one hand and continued to protest herself with the other hand, yet no help came. But when she raised her other hand also, giving up self-protection, help came at once and in abundance. It means that when she surrendered herself completely to the Supreme power, or whatever you may call it, she got full protection against the great calamity perpetrated on her in sheer revengefulness."

Coming to her portrayal of the modern woman, I raised another point, "In *Silapadma* we find two parallel stories of Chandrabhaga, young wife of the chief sculptor of Konark temple, and Prachiprabha a well educated modern researcher, which reveals that despite centuries of gap, these two women are almost identical in their intrinsic nature and the strong bondage of their *sanskaras*. Do you think, the modern Indian woman has not changed much basically inspite of the status of equality bestowed on her by our constitution and the law of the land?"

Highlighting the dilemma of the liberated woman, she observed, "The modern Indian woman is the victim of a terrible conflicting transitional period, torn between two different value systems. Inspite of the status of equality bestowed upon her by our constitution and law she has not changed in the core and is not completely free from the bondage of age-old *Sanskars* because the society is not ready to change overnight along with the law. She is torn between two desires, between the double standards of social norms adopted by the society for men and women. As per statistics the atrocities practised on women, including bride-burning for dowry, rape etc. have increased with the increase of general and female literacy percentage."

She has given a happy ending to her novel concerning the freedom struggle, this led me to question its plausibility, "In *Uttarmarg* you have brought out effectively the predicament of the freedom-fighters after the independence which brought in its wake complete shattering of our long cherished ideals. Why could this novel not have a tragic ending?"

"*Uttarmarg* refers to changing situations and characters and their hopes, aspirations and sufferings, sacrifices for a greater cause, beginning from 1920 till Independence and for sometime beyond. The novel itself has a tragic ending depicting complete shattering of our long-cherished ideals and dreams. Even then the novel has an optimistic touch at the end showing a ray of hope because it was too early to leave hope for a better future after the unparalleled sacrifices of the people of the country."

I probed further, "About a decade has passed since your novel *Uttarmarg* was first published in Oriya. Our basic value system, once eroded has gone from bad to worse with alarming speed. Don't you think that hoping for restoration of basic human values in the present situation would just be a hope against hope? Don't you think, it is hightime that some sort of painful surgery be applied as your Draupadi felt it necessary to save the mankind?"

Realising her over-zealousness, she admitted, "You have rightly remarked that towards the end of my novel I was hoping against hope. I was aware of it. But I thought, let us hope for the best and be prepared for the worst, the painful eventualities you have hinted at."

Then, I took her short stories on the tribal life and asked, "Some of your short stories on the tribal life turn out to be the best picturesque accounts of their way of life, rather than engrossing short stories? What is your concept of a good short story?"

She sensed the implication of my query and replied, "You are right that in my stories on tribal life I have concentrated on giving vivid pictures of their way of life. A story can only be comprehended in its cultural background. My stories on tribal life, based on the most primitive Bonda tribe of Orissa result from my post-doctoral research. The Bondas are very aggressive and impulsive and commit murder any moment. Moreover they remain in inaccessible areas on a mountaineous range. Therefore, my main purpose here was to give a clear picture of their way of life, creating a story out of their simple but savage characteristics. In the process the art of good short story might sometimes get lost."

Concluding the conversation, I asked, "What is your concept of fulfilment as a writer? Many such occasions must have come your way. Will you like to recount a couple of them for us?"

She welcomed the question and went into a reminiscent mood, "Where is fulfilment in the life of a writer? The writer is a dissatisfied, unfulfilled creature in search of words to express her thoughts and feelings. As a women struggles with her own strength and power, struggles against her own flesh and body to give birth to a child, an author's pain is just like that, exclusively her pain. Nobody can understand the labour of heart and brain, nor can the writer explain the pain in words. The curse of a writer is that words fall short and are inadequate to describe and rightly portray the depth of his/her feelings and experiences. So each time after producing a piece of work, something remains unspoken and hence the pain of creation lingers till another creation; again the pain of unexpressed thoughts and feelings. The crystal is so clear, so transparent that words fall short to describe the clarity. Hence crystal is opaque, that is the pain and unfulfilment of a writer.

"Yes, Of course there is a ray of sunlight in a cloudy sky and there are some moments of fulfilment in the life of a writer when the reader's insight sees the clarity of the crystal with the help of the writer's limited words in a fiction or any genre of writing. A writer's aim is achieved when he/she sees that his/her writing has some impact on social behaviour of the readers. I am fortunate enough to have got many such moments of fulfilment, which I would like to share with you.

"I have a story titled *Accident* in which a couple ignored a road accident and did not give lift to the injured in their car, to be removed to the hospital. On reaching their destination they had been sent for by the Superintendent of the hospital to identify a body which was none other than their beloved son. Once a media person came to me on a new year day and expressed his gratitude for helping him in shifting his bossom friend to the hospital from the road; the friend met with an accident while returning on a scooter after the December 31st night's party. The media person was not willing to give him a lift when the crowd requested him and went away. But after a while he remembered my story *Accident* and came back to discover that the person was his bossom friend.

"My story *Abyakt* (Unsaid), telecast in prime time serial EK KAHANI of Delhi Doordarshan, is based on a day to day affair of every house-hold. A poor domestic servant boy has been suspected of theft of a shawl of the 'Babu' bought by the house-wife. The servant boy was asking for a shawl for his old father in the village for the coming winter. This was not complied with by the house-wife. The servant boy went to village on a week's holiday but did not agree to come back. Incidentally, the new shawl of the master was not found in the wardrobe and immediately the servant boy was suspected of theft. The price of the shawl was recovered from the poor father through a relative of the house-wife who was a police officer. After some months the shawl was found in the wordrobe, which had been carelessly kept beneath a typewriter. The repentant house-wife rushed to the village to pay back the poor man's money and to bring back the boy. It was too late. The poor man had died of severe cold and agony of being the father of a thief in the eyes of the villagers which ruined his health immediately after the incident. The boy had left the village being tortured by the villagers for bringing bad name to their village.

"After the story was telecast I got phone call from a house-wife who practically broke down on the other side of the phone and requested me to telecast another episode in which the servant boy is traced and brought back to his master's house with love and care. She told me that her children were crying, seeing the tele-serial, that they decided to go to their servant boy's village taking a blanket for his old father. Their servant was also asking for a blanket for his old father. He left for the village empty-handed as his prayer had not been granted.

"I have a novel *Aparichita* in which the marriage of a girl was not materialised in the last moment. The bridegroom received an anonymous letter which drew a question mark regarding the bride's character. Hence, he refused to come to marry the girl. The girl's life became miserable after that, being branded an unchaste girl. After many years the boy comes to know that the letter was totally baseless and it was sent by a frustrated vagabond who was interested in the girl without her knowledge. The story ends with a tragic touch, with a message to the society. This novel has been filmed and the story got Orissa Government's Award for best film story of the year 1980. But the award is not the point of fulfilment on my part. The point is after the film had been released in rural areas, I got many letters of gratitude from many parents, boys and girls, who wrote to me that the story saved them from breaking their marriages due to anonymous letters in the name of the girls which is a common phenomena in rural Orissa to avenge the girl's father for old family dispute.

"I have a story *Achhuan Dian* (Untouchable God) based on discrimination of human beings on account of caste and religion in Hindu temples. The story is a tragic and touchy one. I got a letter from a village priest who wrote to me that they have allowed the so-called untouchables inside their temple after going through that story."

Her elaborate reaction prompted me to turn to otherside of the coin. I observed, "Thank you very much for sharing with us your moments of fulfilment. What about regrets, if any, as a writer? Would you like to share some?"

Her response was free and frank," My first regret as a writer is that our value system is eroding with an alarming speed and the writer can do almost nothing to arrest the degenerating tendencies. My other regret is the inadequacy of the tools, the language, the word, at my disposal as a writer to express myself fully. Everytime after completing a piece of work pain of the unexpressed, much more than the joy of the expressed, lingers on till the next creation."

(New Delhi—5.5.1994)

*

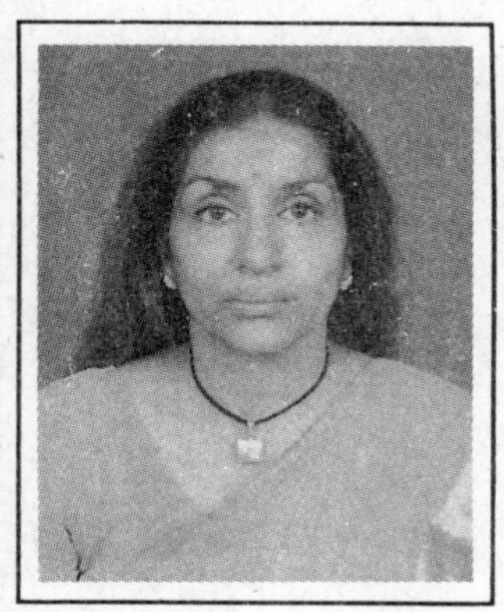

Lakshmi Kannan (Kāveri)

B. 13.8.1947, Mysore, *mt.* Tamil, *Edn.* M.A., Ph.D., *Car.* Teaching, taught English in Jadavpur University and also in colleges at Delhi & Calcutta, now a freelance writer, *Hons.* Honorary Fellow in Writing, University of Iowa, USA—1987, British Council Visitor, England—1992, Writer-in-Residence on a Charles Wallace Trust Fellowship, University of Kent, England—1993, Regional Judge for URASIA, Commonwealth Writer's Prize, London,—1995, *Pubs. Tamil short stories Osaigal* (Sounds)—1984, *Venmai Porthiyathu* (Covered in White)—1992, *Inru Maalai, Ennudan* (With Me, This Evening)—1993, *novel Athukku Poganum* (Going Home)—1986, *English Poetry Impressions*—1974, *The Glow and the Grey*—1976, *Exiled Gods*—1985, *short stories* (in translation) *Rhythms*—1986, *Parijat and Other Stories*—1992, *India Gate and Other Stories*—1993, *Hindi* (in translation) *Layabaddha* (Rhythm)—1990, *Parten* (Layers)—1996; her short stories have been translated in other Indian languages also. She is also a translator and has extensively translated in English, fiction and poetry, both her own and the works of other eminent Tamil writers.

Fathoming the Human Psyche

Lakshmi Kannan has carved for her a place among the modern women writers of eminence, who delve deep into the psyche of the women caught up between the two conflicting worlds of tradition and modernity, transcending the narrow confines of Feminism. She is a bilingual writer who writes both in English and Tamil. She writes her poems and literary criticisms in English and her fiction in her mother-tongue Tamil under the pseudonym of Kāveri.

In her poems as also in her fiction, one finds a harmonious marriage of modernity with age-old orthodoxy. Through her writings she explores the complexities of human behaviour, how men and women confront themselves in the face of the inner compulsions and the challenges posed by the day to day stresses and strains in the changing social and economic situations, and gradually involves herself in the subtleties of the changing profile of women and the present wilderness of human relations.

About the emergence of her poetry she says that her poems sometimes originate in a visual experience as she is extremely sensitive to the pictorial quality of words and ideas, and to colours also. This way she refers perhaps to the intuitive aspect of her poetry. While conscious reasoning is verbal, intuition operates non-verbally through iconic imagery, stored economically in this form in the prelogical areas of our subconscious. The verbal stage comes in later when the poetry starts pouring out in the form of a poem.

Recounting her intense struggle during her creative act, she observes, "There is a luminous something that glimers and beckons from a distance. Still in a nascent state, it threatens to dissolve any moment, to merge again in the fleeting, amorphous life around it. It is a point that excites a story to take shape within the crucible of a consciousness that is anxious to capture this 'something' in its true lights, in mid-flight as it were. With that begins the lonely, uncertain search of a writer when she decides on how much to tell and how much to hold back unsaid, tossing as she does on the dialectics of a wish to assert herself as a writer, running counter to a more luxurious wish to simply surrender to her subject in silence."

In her short story *Genesis* she explores the concept of a story, "But what's a story? It is something real. And there are stories after stories after stories. With all the colours of the real. Colours that elude in life but condense with stark reality in a story, or a photograph. And if the story endures and is honoured by time, the illusion is complete—for the reader, for the author. The illusion has permanence before there is a fade-out."

She has made a mark as a critic also. Her doctoral research work on Saul Bellow has been widely appreciated. She takes a keen interest in the sociology of literature and has presented several papers in seminars at home and abroad.

I was drawn to her writings for their incisiveness and had an in-depth interview with her on her creative endeavours.

I started the ball rolling with the first question: "You have written poems as well as short stories and novelettes. But what would you like to be remembered as—a poet, a fictionist or a critic—and why?" She quipped, "I would like to be remembered as a poet and fiction writer."

I probed further and asked, "But Why?"

She elaborated, "To me, as far as writing goes, a poem or a story or what gets into a novel seems to come so spontaneously, appears to come almost involuntarily, almost unwilled. So it is very precious for me, the experience of something that taps on my consciousness that I go to write. I have also written quite a few critical articles and presented them in many seminars. It seems to be more deliberate effort, a more consciously undertaken effort."

We find her fiction in English, translated from the original Tamil, but her poetry appears to have dawned upon her in English direct. This prompted me to find out the reason for this differentiation and I remarked, "It is believed that things closer to one's heart find spontaneous expression in one's mother tongue and those close to head may come out in the second language. But yours seems to be a different case, Tamil being your mother tongue. Would you like to elucidate?"

She responded sharply, "I find it difficult to agree that poetry comes close to the heart and that fiction comes close to the head. I think both poetry and fiction are close to the heart and head alike, and equally so. Both are spontaneously created, although fiction may call for more details and specifics.

"To answer your question about why I write poetry in English and fiction in Tamil, the honest answer would be that it just happened to fall into a pattern that way. That is about all. As a young girl, I began writing poetry in English. There was a lot of English around me, in the milieu I moved in. Also, I was teaching English and researching in English and American studies, which I suppose can give one an overdose of the language.

"Then, when I began to write fiction —and that was a little later—I wrote a couple of stories in English. Fiction involves 'actual' people with names, identifiably demographic details, geocultural features and so on. I experimented with the idea of writing the same stories in Tamil and realised that the whole atmosphere was transformed. The same characters who spoke in English, when I made them speak in Tamil, instantly seemed to find a linguistic climate within which they could speak, act, behave and move about much more freely, naturally and spontaneously than they did in English. Tamil seemed to tap them alive somehow and they opened out for me. Moreover, characters from the kind of background which you don't normally associate with English, characters such as very old women or men who have not received any formal education in English, characters from the interiors of villages and small towns, and characters from other walks of life who don't use English in their everyday lives, but who are nevertheless strong and articulate in their own languages, people such as servants, vendors, gardeners, street children and others—these are the kinds of characters who respond beautifully when touched by Tamil.

"I then realised a change coming over me. I just began to enjoy the experience of writing in Tamil tremendously. I enjoyed living in the speech rhythms, the patterns, the natural rise and fall of the language, its richness and, of course, not foregoing its bitter, acerbic, hurtful wit and humour, so inherent in the language. Now I enjoy writing in Tamil as much as I enjoy writing in English".

Turning to her short stories, I asked, "Delving deep into the psyche of your characters, mainly the females, your fiction never fails to raise pertinent questions agitating our male-oriented society. But your stories like *Thirteen Days After, With Me, This Evening, Sweet Reasonableness* prompt me to ask you about the role of craft in fiction as you conceive it."

She inquired, "Any particular reason why these three stories have been singled out?" I explained, "I picked up these stories for their ending. To me they could have ended in a more striking manner." She sought further clarification, "Is it that you did not like the way they concluded or the conclusion was not effective?"

I added, "I believe, when a story reaches its point of culmination it must click and end quickly without dragging. The end must impress strikingly. The endings, not the end, of these stories do not appeal to me that way."

She conceded, "Perhaps you have a point there, because I cannot judge with the degree of objectivity it requires. Nor do I feel that a critic is entirely objective. But I must add that when I write a story I am not conscious of when, where and how it would end. I surrender myself to the forces within the story. I do not bring about an end of my liking. I allow them to conclude in their own way. Maybe you are right."

While studying her short stories I had sensed a strong pro- Feministic leaning in them. So I observed, "Your acute concern for the plight of women in our decadent society touches at times the chords of Feminism which tend to encourage reactionary attitudes culminating in revengefulness, as in stories like *India Gate*. Don't you think that to be natural and genuine literature has to transcend all the 'isms'?"

She retorted, "May I ask, Dr. Rangra, whether your reaction is based on the specific male point of view?" I assured her, "Oh no, not at all. I do appreciate the content of the story and went along as a reader with three-forth of it. But I was, if I may say, disappointed towards the end, because that gave me the impression that solution lies in separation as there is no other go, and that worries me as a member of society, not as a male exclusively."

She asserted, "But for Padmini there was no way except to step out of marriage."

Turning to the deeper implication of this approach, I remarked, "Does it mean that in the marriages where couples find themselves unable to carry on together the only solution lies is stepping out of marriage? I feel, if we accept this as the only solution, even the newly wed couples would exercise no patience to give it enough time for a fair trial and would jump to the conclusion that they must come out of the wed-lock."

Reacting frankly, she said, "I totally agree with your anxiety about this negativism in their reaction and that is not very Indian too. But as far as this story goes, Padmini feels that she has invested enough in the marriage and that they are not only incompatible, he is a borderline case of barbaric behaviour that he tries to establish which is no longer acceptable. I would rather go as far as saying that it should not be accepted. But if you reverse the situation where it is not the woman who is the victim, but it is the husband who is the sufferer, then I would admit that the Feminism which you have aptly questioned is not something to be celebrated, as it has let down its own members. If you take it that way you have a crop of aggressive, predatory, bitter women who have victimised their husbands. In that case, I would be the first one to take side against them. By the way, the ending of this story was appreciated by a large number of Tamil and English readers".

Elucidating my premise, I asked, "I don't think that to counter the male-chauvinism in our society the only alternative left with the woman is to go for female-chauvinism. It would be a revengeful approach only which the protagonists of Feminism press for. But may I ask, did this reactionary approach succeed in solving the problem? A mature thinking is now developing as the reactionary phase appears to be over. More and more women are now coming to realise that if the decadent institution of marriage is to be revolutionised, the revolution will have to be worked out from within, not by renouncing or denouncing it, though it may entail lot of suffering and sacrifice by both the partners, if not in their own interest, in the interest of their children at least. I express this concern not as a male, but as a member of the society".

Reacting favourably, she said, "I totally agree with your positive approach. But in this particular story Padmini feels that she has been driven to the wall and left with no option other than stepping out. In many of my other stories there are quite a few protagonists who work out equations within their families, make compromises and come to peace not on their own terms, but in the larger interest of the family.

"Yes, in general you are absolutely right. Genuine literature has to transcend all 'isms'. Feminism *per se* may strike you as partisan, but like you observed in earlier question, women have obviously been at a terrible disadvantages for a long time now. They have had a raw deal. So when I take up these issues, I also take them up as 'Human right Issues'.

"However, it is a fact that I have written a lot of stories in which the central character is a male. This provides a balance to my approach."

Then. I referred to another trend in her writing and observed, "Some of your fictional pieces like *Sable Shadows at the Witching Time of Night* turn out to be good character sketches. Couldn't these be woven into well-rounded stories. I Wonder?"

She replied, "There is a trend in English which is called 'Faction', i.e., Fact + Fiction. In this format a writer uses his/her fictional skills to narrate something that has actually happened. He may not disguise his name or the names of his other characters just as he may acknowledge the actual locale, situation, time and so on. I wanted to try out this format. I received a mixed reaction, but in Tamil the story got a very positive response. I could have, of course, easily and elaborately pretended that the situation was "all fiction" by giving everyone, including myself, fictional names, but what would be the purpose of it?"

Touching upon a recent controversy, I remarked, "Some people, mainly female writers, feel that male writers are not able to do justice to their female characters as they fail to understand them fully. Do you find any substance in this contention?"

She reacted sharply, "No, I don't subscribe to this view. Some of the best male writers such as T. Janakiraman and 'Kalki' in Tamil, Saratchandra Chattopadhyay and Rabindranah Tagore in Bangla, have given readers some unforgettable women characters. It all depends on how just, how unbiased a male writer is, but equally on how generous he is, on how sensitive and fair-minded he is regarding women. This will certainly show in the quality of his women characters and, of course, in the general overall quality of his writings."

Looking for a personal touch in her writings, I asked, "It is believed that all creative writings are essentially autobiographical in one way or the other. Which one of your stories reflect you the most?"

She replied, "All creative writings are not autobiographical in the strict literal sense of the term. On the contrary, a writer gets a clearer perspective if he/she is a little detached from his/her subject. Because writing processes reality in subtle ways that may go well beyond the author! Even if a writer begins on a personal note, she will eventually distance herself from the experience portrayed so that she can do full justice to, not the 'facts' but the inner truth. Which of my stories reflect me the most? It is difficult to point out. Perhaps a few such as *The Maze, Rhythms* (I have actually witnessed a scene like that in a temple in Madras) and some others."

Lakshmi Kannan has made a mark as a translator also. So I observed, "You have indulged yourself profusely in rendering translations which to me is a challenging task. But much more challenging is the venture of translating one's own creative writings and curbing the urge to retouch the original. How do you manage to maintain the self-restraint expected from a translator?"

She admitted, "I do realize that I have done a considerable amount of translation. It all began with a demand from editors of magazines, then book publishers and so on. Although I looked around for a translator, I did not succeed in finding anybody.

"Yes, it calls for a great restraint while translating one's own work because there is always a temptation to improve. The itch of the pen, I guess! But I get the same impulse even when I am translating someone else's work. So either way, one has to be restrained, hold oneself in check and strictly adhere to the original text. When I am called upon to translate my work, I take care to put in a gap of time between the original work and my translation. This gives me a distance. I don't translate anything in a hurry."

I probed further, "You have mentioned in 'The Translator's Note" in your book entitled *India Gate* that 'when a translator also happens to be the author, he can get curious feeling of rewriting the original in his search for the closest approximation to the original text, because he knows exactly what he meant when he wrote the original'. I believe that any author-translator's claim that 'he knows exactly what he meant when he wrote the original' is the product of the conscious, whereas the content and the import of the original text belongs to the subconscious, the realm of the creative act. Many writers admit that they write in a trance or under some sort of a spell and cannot pinpoint why and what they wrote or what they meant when they wrote. Thus, the so-called right of the author-translator to retouch or recast the original text is, I believe, questionable.

"This issue may be examined from author's angle also. The author's experience during the act of creation is one compact unit of experience to be viewed in totality and not piecemeal. The author-translator's experience of the same original text is another unit of experience, particularly when undertaken after a gap of time. The two units of experience need not be identical essentially just because the experiencer happens to be one and the same person. It is very likely that the flaw spotted by the author-translator in the original text which he is tempted to remove sprang from viewing the original in fragmentation, instead of experiencing it in totality as he did when he wrote the original. This leads me to believe again that the author-translator has no right to retouch the original. Would you like to comment?"

She responded frankly, "I find this very reassuring after I heard you about the imagined flaw, an afterthought of finding a flaw. Whether the author has a flaw or if it is only an imagined flaw, it can be determined only after examining the experience of the original in totality since it is a compact unit of experience to be viewed as a whole as you have rightly mentioned. After I have heard you, I feel, the author should not look back upon his earlier writings from this angle, since that would serve no purpose.

"Secondly, you dispute the claim of the author that he or she knows exactly what he meant when he wrote the original. You are probably right. The original mood is no longer there when she was urged to write, she had to write, was rather possessed to write. Thus, while translating her own writings she must take the stance of a translator like any other translator".

Trying to find out how the translation of her works were received by the reader, I asked, "Many of your writings have been translated into Hindi and many are on the way. Since you can understand Hindi I venture to ask you whether they succeed in giving the readers a feel of the original? How have the Hindi translations been received *vis-a-vis* the English translations of your works?"

Welcoming the question, she replied, "It is a very tricky question. All I can say is that there is a world of difference. My experience with the Hindi reader has been heart-warming in the case of both my poetry and story collections published by Bharatiya Jnanpith and Birla Foundation. I receive readers reactions in the form of tiny postcards from the remote districts of entire Hindi belt—Haryana, Punjab, Uttar Pradesh, Bihar etc. and from people with different professions, not the literary guys. They understand the story in letter as well as in spirit just because it is in Hindi. This is a unique experience which I am unlikely to get from the upper class English readers, because I know the kind of response I get from them. This is qualitatively very different and to me very precious. Similar is the experience when my writings get translated in Marathi, Bengali and occasionally in Gujarati. That gives me the feeling that I am reaching my own people".

Then, I turned to another aspect of indulging in translation work, "Do you enjoy translating your own works? Don't you feel that the time and energy consumed by this arduous task could be better channelised into creative writing?" Her reply was: "Now I am tired of translating my own works and I am not going to do it anymore. It does consume a lot of my time and energy which can be better spent in creative pursuits".

Coming to her poetry, I touched upon the inner process of her creative act and asked, "You have mentioned that many of your poems originated in visual experience. In your venture to capture the visual image and to develop it into a poem, you must have felt miserable many a time when the word, the only tool a poet can wield, instead of expressing you fully and faithfully, betrays you by way of deceptive, secondary elaborations. Would you care to share with us any one of such experiences with reference to a particular poem of yours?"

Finding it difficult to pinpoint her inner processes in composing a poem, she remarked, "Poetry is a seductive medium. It has its treacheries. A poet enjoys letting herself into its uncertainties. No, developing a visual image does not leave me in misery all the time, except perhaps in instances where I totally fail to communicate in a poem. But a visual element for poetry is a strong incentive to explore. As for the deceptive, secondary elaborations, any second, or third reading of a draft mercilessly expose these to my own eyes. So, I don't let them creep into my final script. I still go by the tried and tested method of writing something that I insist on calling my 'first draft', however personally satisfying it may be, and then putting it away for a few days before giving it a 'once over' again. Then all the flaws seem to be visible; so I set to re-work on the poem again."

Then, I took up another issue, that is, the impact of poetry when it goes along with visual illustration: "In your anthology entitled 'Exiled Gods", illustrations go along with each poem. Maybe these illustrations help the reader, but don't you think that any illustration that goes with a poem tends to restrict its appeal to a particular point of view and curb independent comprehension?"

She replied, "The illustrations are essentially an artist's perception of the poems and therefore reflect just one point of view. I think few readers go by the illustrations. In my experience, they just take one glance at the illustration after which they are on their own. That is why it may not be restrictive to have illustrations occasionally. They stimulate up to a point but other than that, they have a limited role. The reader is all on his own."

Comparing her recent poems with earlier ones, I observed, "Your recent poems such as *Family Tree* and *I Take the Shape of* are superb in bringing out the plight of the Indian woman in a highly suggestive manner. Is it because of the deft use of the symbols or because here you have transcended the barriers of Feminism which dominated many of your earlier poems?"

She replied, "An interesting question. Just as I mentioned earlier that even an autobiographical note has to be processed by the creativity of writing, I feel strongly that a woman's feministic ideas need to be equally processed and objectified by creativity on its own terms, not on her terms. Only then can it reach the level of art. If I have succeeded in the two poems you have mentioned, it may be because I allcw a subject to take its course, to take its form and shape and do not let my own ideas interfere with the work. Increasingly, this is my attitude to my writings. I, or my 'feminist' ideas, should not condition my writing. Rather, I should surrender myself completely to my subject and let it take its own course."

My concluding question was, "What is your concept of fulfilment as a writer? Many such occasions must have come your way. Would you like to share some with us?"

In a relaxed mood she replied, "I like to experiment with forms. I like to take risks even if it means losing out on my 'tried and tested' readers. But when I get sensitive and intelligent response even to this experimental mode of writing, and I am understood for what I have tried, then I feel truly fulfilled. It is this live, symbiotic relationship with an intelligent, discerning reader which gives me fulfilment. Another deeply satisfying experience is reading great books, books that lift you out of yourself. Then it does not seem to matter that I am spending time reading a book, instead of writing my own stuff."

(New Delhi—20.01.1996)

*